SELF-DIRECTED
LEARNING:

EMERGING THEORY & PRACTICE

Huey B. Long and Associates

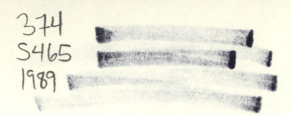

International Standard Book Number ISBN 0-9622488-0-0
Library of Congress Catalog Card Number 89-611107

CONTENTS

iii

TABLES AND FIGURES

Tables

Figures

v

Preface

Self-Directed Learning: Emerging Theory and Practice is based on selected papers presented at the Second North American Symposium on Adult Self-Directed Learning held at the University of Oklahoma, March, 1988.   The two-day symposium was sponsored by the Oklahoma Research Center for Continuing Professional and Higher Education.   Approximately one-half of the papers presented at the conference were selected for publication.

The papers represent the work of scholars from Canada and the United States from Florida to Wisconsin, from Tennessee to Oklahoma, and from Texas to Georgia. The annual symposium on adult self-directed learning is becoming recognized as the place to discuss new developments and ideas concerning self-directed learning. Restrictions that limit papers to original work not previously reported provide scholars with an opportunity to quickly report their research while others have an equally desirable opportunity to learn about the latest research. The symposia are attended by advanced scholars of self-directed learning as well as graduate students who are beginning their research into related questions.

The papers reported in chapter format here were selected for publication for several reasons. Some of the chapters develop fresh approaches to conceptualizing self-direction in adult learning. Others report new research findings and/or employ research methods not used frequently in self-directed learning research. Brief comments about each chapter follow.

Chapter one, Self-Directed Learning: Emerging Theory and Practice is an overview of an emerging concept of self-directed learning.   The concept as developed by Long emphasizes the psychological aspects of self-direction in contrast to the sociological thrust that places a premium on solitary or independent learning activity.

Chapter two, Self-Directed Orientation Toward Learning: A Learning Style?, by Adrianne Bonham, conceptualizes three possible learning styles associated with a self-directed learning orientation: other directed learning style, self-directed learning style according to the instructional mode, and self-directed learning style according to the inquiry mode.

vii

In chapter three John Peters raises some questions about Reasoning, Problem Solving and Thinking as Correlates of Self-Direction in Learning. He also discusses a methodology that has promise for the investigation of processes of self-direction.

Chapter four, Facilitating Self-Direction in Learning: Not a Contradiction of Terms, by Randy Garrison, introduces the provocative idea that ability is required for learner control in the learning process. Three dimensions of control (independence, power and support) are examined in the context of self-directed learning.

Chapter five, The Development and Field-Testing of an Adult Basic Education Form of the Self-Directed Learning Readiness Scale, by Lucy Gulielmino reports on her work to develop an assessment instrument for use with adult basic education students. The ABE version is different from the original SDLRS in several ways: the reading level was reduced to make it appropriate for the population, and the response options were simplified, according to Guglielmino. Procedures employed in the development of the SDLRS-ABE are described and discussed.

Chapter six, Self-Directed Learning Among Clinical Laboratory Scientists: A Closer Look at the OCLI, by Carol McCoy and Michael Langenbach examines the learning behavior of clinical laboratory scientists. They also analyze the Oddi Continuing Learning Inventory through factor analysis.

Chapter seven, A Meta-Analytic Study of the Relationship between Adult Self-Direction in Learning and Psychological Well-Being: A review of the Research from 1977 to 1987, by Sandra McCune and Gonzalo Garcia, Jr., provides a meta-analysis of the research.

Chapter eight, Bridging Theory and Practice, by Judith DeJoy and Helen Mills describes the development of a Personal Learning Lab that emphasizes self-direction in learning. According to the authors, the activities of the learning lab provide additional opportunities for studying the concept and theory of self-directed learning.

Chapter ten, Truth Unguessed and Yet to be Discovered, written by Long is based on the analysis of a biography of Sir Wilder Penfield, the famed neurosurgeon. Long suggests that Penfield's propensity for self-directed learning may be traced to his early childhood.

It should be apparent from the above brief description of the ten chapters that they differ in interesting and important ways while exhibiting some critical areas of agreement. One of the most stimulating areas of consensus concerns the interest in psychological control. The chapters by Bonham, Garrison, Long and Peters are more explicit on this point while the work of Guglielmino, McCoy and Langenbach and McCune and Garcia are supportive. This idea implies that the learner can manifest self-direction in learning independent of the learning context or environment providing certain fundamental conditions, such as learner ability, exist. Such a premise should be amenable to empirical investigation. We look forward to learning of the results of research designed to test the premise.

Huey B. Long
January, 1989

Chapter One

SELF-DIRECTED LEARNING: EMERGING THEORY AND PRACTICE

Huey B. Long

The idea of individual responsibility for learning is not limited to current thought. It has a rich and lengthy history, however, scholars and others have been slow to develop a systematic inquiry into personal control and responsibility for learning. Even educators of adults, who enthusiastically embrace the concepts of self-teaching (Tough, 1971) and self-directed learning have directed their energies to questions of theory, research procedures and application in a capricious and inconsistent manner. Numerous investigations concerning adult self-directed learning have been conducted and reported in the past decade as more researchers have become interested in the topic. Nevertheless, conceptual difficulties and differences continue to complicate communications and application efforts.

Two developments are encouraging. First, the annual North American Symposium on Adult Self-Directed Learning appears to be stimulating researchers while also providing a showcase for current research reports. Second, a shift in ways of thinking about self-directed learning seems to be occurring. The shift is a movement from a narrow view of self-directed learning that is based upon the pedagogical and social nature of learning, e.g., conceptualizing self-directed learning as something that an individual does in social isolation.

Current interest in adult self-direction in learning appears to be associated with the work of Malcolm Knowles and Allen Tough. Tough's work in adults' learning projects on self-teaching emerged from the earlier work of Cyril Houle (Houle, 1988). Knowles' influential ideas concerning self-direction in learning as reported in the early 1970's seem to have been derived from his earlier YMCA activities and European concepts of andragogy.

More recently Stephen Brookfield has emerged as a major authority on self-directed learning. His various positions (Brookfield, 1984, 1985, 1987) on adult self-direction in learning, however, have not been particularly helpful in clarifying the concept. Nevertheless, Brookfield, Knowles and Tough seem to be preoccupied with pedagogical aspects of adult self-directed learning to the near exclusion of psychological elements.

Elsewhere, (Long 1986, 1988) I have suggested that adult self-directed learning has a number of conceptual dimensions. In some cases the sociological dimension has been dominant. In this kind of situation self-directed learning is defined by the social isolation of the learner. Another definition emerges from a pedagogical emphasis, (Knowles prefers androgogy to pedagogy, nevertheless the actions are similar) e.g., diagnosing learning needs, setting learning objectives, identifying resources, and evaluating learning (Knowles, 1975). A third definition resides in a psychological concept, e.g., the mental activities of the learner.

Let us look at each of the three conceptual dimensions. Perhaps the most popular usage of the term self-directed learning applies to the sociological dimension. As a consequence self-directed learning is equated with independent learning. Unfortunately, independent learning also has two dimensions: (a) physical separation or isolation of the learner and (b) interpersonal power. According to the first of these conditions the independent learner is a solitary learner. As a result of the primary use of the sociological dimension self-directed learning is defined as learning that occurs in isolation, e.g. correspondence study, computer assisted instruction and so forth are examples of this notion. According to the notion of interpersonal power as provided in the second dimension the independent learner is an autonomous learner (also, often a solitary learner) for whom the parameters and learning activities are personally established. When problems are encountered the learner may consult with some perceived expert and consider the information free of any coercion to accept the information. Both of the ideas tend to stress possible solitary behavior. They also ignore pedagogical distinctiveness and the psychological implications of each concept. More will be said on this point later.

The second popular conception of self-directed learning is forcused on a pedagogical model. Accordingly, self-directed learning emphasizes pedagogical procedures carried out by the learner referred to in Tough's (1967) early work as self-teaching. Here the degree to which learning is self-directed is determined by the freedom to which the learner is given to set learning goals, to identify and use resources, to determine the effort and time to be allocated to learning and to decide how and what kind of evaluation of the learning will take place. According to this view sociological isolation of the learner is not required, neither must the learner be completely autonomous. As a result, according to this concept, it is believed that self-directed learning may take place within group learning frameworks, institutionally sponsored or otherwise. This idea contributes to thinking about the third dimension.

The final dimension to be discussed here is the psychological dimension. This concept flows most directly from the second dimension mentioned above, but is not identical with it. Actually, each of the previous dimensions, except the social-psychological one, and their various manifestations generally ignore the psychological process. This is amazing when learning is basically a psychological event. Note, both of the sociological conceptualization (isolation and autonomy) of self-directed learning emphasizes the pedagogical activities, e.g. setting learning goals, identifying resources, evaluating the learning and so fourth. The main difference between the sociological conceptualizations is the initiator of the pedagogical procedures. Remember the observation made earlier that discussion of the sociological models failed to consider pedagogical distinctiveness. In the first, the isolated learner is basically operating under a guided curriculum developed by someone other than the learner whereas the autonomous or independent learner is not pedagogically constrained by a curriculum developed by the authority of an institution or a specific agent. Perhaps the main constraints on autonomous learners reside in their cognitive ability, the authority of the discipline (or content), knowledge of the topic and their psychological bent toward nonconformity, skepticism and critical thought. Thus, the two sociological views of self-directed learning imply the possibility that some pedagogical processes are common to both while ignoring their differences. The second major mode, e.g. the pedagogical model clearly focuses primarily on the relationship of the learner to the pedagogical process and only secondarily on the social relationship of learners to authority figures. The degree of isolation or physical independence of the learner is not critical to the definition. The critical element is the amount of freedom the learner has to influence the pedagogical process. In summary, both dimensions of the sociological model and the pedagogical model seem to emphasize the importance of the pedagogical model. In the former the sociological characteristics are most important. In the latter, the pedagogical model emphasizes the importance of the pedagogical process. The basic pedagogical procedures common to the three concepts discussed thus far seem to be similar to the pedagogical procedures of traditional learning. If this is the case, what, is critical to self-directed learning?

The critical dimension in self-directed learning is not the sociological variable, nor it is the pedagogical factor. The main distinction is the psychological variable, that is the degree to which the learner, or the self, maintains active control of the learning process. Kasworm (1988) expresses the idea as follows: "... the learner has consciously accepted the responsibility to make decisions, to be one's own learning change agent, rather than abrogating the responsibility to external sources or authorities" (p. 69). Accordingly the learner may be self-directing in either of the two sociological frameworks, guided independent activity or autonomous action, as well as the pedagogical condition. For example, the learner can be psychologically self-directing in the sociologically autonomous model, the sociologically solitary one or in a situation characteristic of the pedagogical model. Conversely, if learners are not psychologically self-directing they are unlikely to engage in the autonomous learning activity and are likely to be unsuccessful learners in the solitary learning modality. Similar lack of success is predicted for the psychologically passive learner in the pedagogical model.

Table 1.1: An Illustrative Relationship Among Kinds of Learning in Order of the Probability of Self-Directed Learning Occurring.

I	II	III
Autonomous Learning	Pedagogical Self-Directed Learning	Traditional Institutional Settings
(may be individual)	(individual or group)	(correspondence computer study, asserted instruction)

Therefore, <u>psychological</u> <u>self-directedness</u>, or <u>psychological control is the necessary and sufficient cause for self-directed learning</u>. In contrast the other models discussed here may be neither a sufficient nor necessary cause.

All other things being equal we could, therefore, suggest that autonomous learning, the kind of learning studied by Allen Tough (1967) contains the greatest likelihood for psychological self-direction in contrast with pedagogical direction as illustrated in Table 1:1. However, as most educators are more keenly interested in learning that occurs within an institutional framework attention is now directed to what I call pedagogical self-directed learning.

Pedagogical self-directed learning emerges from the interaction of psychological control and pedagogical control. When each of the forms of control are equal or when psychological control exceeds pedagogical control (of a teacher, tutor, etc.) we can describe the situation as a self-directed learning condition. When pedagogical control is excessive and the learner's psychological control is limited learning becomes other-directed.

Let me suggest how psychological control can vary even within constant pedagogically controlled conditions. Assume we are in an adult classroom where the instructor favors learner responsibility for learning e.g., learner initiative and self motivated learning. In this classroom the instructor provides an environment where individual learning goals are negotiated, appropriate resources and activities are individually selected by the students and a process of evaluation is mutually agreed upon by the instructor and the student. Even in this situation we will discover some learners who cannot or will not assume psychological control. They will passively await guidance if not commands from the instructor, they will not <u>critically</u> assess the resources, they will not reevaluate their own presuppositions, or

4

assumptions, etc. These learners will also become very frustrated with the instructor. Now let us look at a situation where the instructor is convinced that ideas about learner responsibility for learning are poppy-cock. This instructor is well organized, systematic, or highly rigid. Course objectives are precise, a required list of reading is provided and there is no consideration of evaluation other than the instructor's secret procedure. Can self-directed learning occur in such a setting? Yes, even though we might not normally identify the class method as a self-directed learning activity that does not <u>prevent</u> some students from maintaining psychological self-control. They may choose from among the course objectives and give <u>relative attention and emphasis</u> to those that are of most interest to them. They may ignore, partially or completely, some of the items on the reading list. They may supplement their reading by additional materials and engage in other subversive learning activities such as devising questions that challenge the authoritative resources. Then, even though the pedagogical controls have placed extreme constraints on the learner's options the creative and psychologically strong learner maintains considerable control while the psychologically weaker learner passively submits. The psychologically weaker learner does not quit the course, because it takes some psychological strength to make that choice.

In summation we can observe that while it may be stimulating and provocative to subscribe to the idea that self-direction in learning is a function of external conditions such as the physical isolation of the learner or the degree to which an instructor yields authority such ideas deal more with pedagogy than psychology. Emphasis on pedagogical procedures to the neglect of psychological process is a dead-end approach to studying self-direction in learning. Pedagogical procedures whether imposed by a teacher or freely chosen by the learner remain pedagogical or "teaching" activities. Hence we have other-teaching or perhaps self-teaching but not self-learning. Self-learning or self-directed learning if you prefer, occurs only when the learner primarily controls the learning (cognitive) processes. The degree of control over the pedagogical procedure is a secondary consideration.

While we have some general agreement on the pedagogical procedures that are appropriate to self-directed learning, we are less aware of the psychological control mechanisms or process.

Garrison (in press) has hinted at the problem with his useful concept of control. While it appears Garrison's ideas regarding control were stimulated by his dissatisfaction with the concept of independent learning as used in distance education they are instructive to the discussion of self-directed learning. For Garrison, control is a result of the interaction of (a) learner independence, (b) learner proficiency and (c) support. He describes proficiency as follows:

Proficiency represents the <u>psychological dimension of control</u>, and therefore covers not only learning skills and ability, but motivation and confidence to persist and succeed (p. 29). (Italics mine)

Furthermore, according to Garrison, the traditional educational relationship includes an interaction among teacher, student and content. These three elements in the pedagogical relationship can be represented by overlapping circles with the area common to all three constituting the area of control. The relationship in Garrison's model is further influenced by the communication element. If I interpret the following statement correctly Garrison conceptualizes control as a pedagogical element. He says

--- control is not transferred automatically to a student solely by giving freedom of choice as to time and place of learning without consideration of the students' abilities and resources. Control is <u>negotiated</u> continuously through sustained interaction (p. 33) (Italics mine)

My views differ from Garrison's on the <u>negotiated</u> aspect of control, at least psychological control. I agree that a teacher's pedagogical control can be negotiated. And I may be splitting semantic hairs here, but I question if the learner's psychological control is negotiable. Granted the learner may <u>accept</u> or <u>buy-into</u> an instructor's pedagogical scheme and thereby proceed in concert with the instructional plan. But, its difficult to imagine the learner <u>negotiating</u> away or giving up creativity, critical analysis, and systematic meta-cognitive procedures. The negotiation may deal with more surface procedures but not deep mental processing activities. Despite this difference, Garrison's ideas are informative and particularly useful in understanding distance education and some of the nuances of self-directed learning.

Writing on student freedom in the public school Rich (1986) also makes some parallel comments. Rather then using control and independence as his theme however, he uses freedom. He discusses two kinds of freedom, (a) freedom from... and (b) freedom to.... Freedom from is defined as "an absence of restraint or coercion so that any restrictions on the individual will be an abrogation of the person's freedom" (p. 125). Freedom to is an extension of freedom from to include the requirement that for an individual to have freedom to do something, the individual must have the ability to perform the act he or she is free to perform. The ideas seems to be similar to Garrison's concept of proficiency.

Rich's discussion leads to the premise that "freedom to" in education leads to cognitive autonomy based on reflective thinking, personal and independent judgements concerning both thought and action coupled with morality and consideration for others. If I have interpreted him correctly, Rich appears to be suggesting that psychological control is nurtured in pedagogical settings that emphasize "freedom to."

Lest some continue to believe that the learner actually has little or no psychological control over learning a few supportive observations from reputable scholars such as Gagne' (1985) follows.

Using an information processing model of learning Gagne' identifies two major cognitive structures that are of interest here: executive control and expectancies. Executive control and expectancies as conceptualized by Gagne' are a portion of long term memory and are themselves learned processes. Their function is to select or determine the particular kinds of information processing in which the learner engages for particular kinds of learning tasks. Furthermore, both of the controlling processes are capable of affecting any and all of the phases of information flow: sensory registration, short-term memory, long-term memory response generation. These processes, according to Gagne' are equivalent to the mathemagenic activities described by Rothkopf (1970) and self-management behaviors referred to by Skinner (1968). Cognitive strategies are also frequently referred to by Brunner (1971). Other scholars (Atkinson and Shriffren, 1968, Grenno and Bjork, 1973) also make prominent use of control processes in models of information-processing theories of learning and memory.

"Expectancies represent the specific motivation of learners to reach the goal of learning that has been set for them or that they have set for themselves," according to Gagne' (1985, p. 78 italics mine). It is assumed that what learners intend to accomplish can influence what they pay attention to, how they encode the learned information, and how their responses are organized. Expectancies are not stable. They are dynamic and continuously oriented toward goal accomplishment thus allowing the learner to select outputs at each information processing stage.

The importance of these concepts to the thesis of this paper is revealed best by quoting Gagne'.

> It is apparent...that learning and remembering cannot be fully accounted for in terms of a simple diagram of information flow. There must also be processes by which the learner selects the nature of processing at each of the stages...How the attention of the learner is directed, how the information is encoded, how it is retrieved, and how it is expressed in organized responses are all matters that require a choice of strategies. This choice is the function of the executive control processes, including expectancies established before the learning is undertaken. The processes have the effect of making the learner a truly intelligent being - one who can learn to learn,' and therefore one who can engage in a large measure of self-instruction. (Gagne' 1985, p. 79)

While the thoughts of Piaget (1970) in this area of self-regulating mechanisms are more obscure than Gagne's he does provide some interesting supportive suggestions. According to Piaget (1972) human thought includes "inborn unconsciousness of thought itself" (p. 144). Yet as human beings mature they can develop a remedy for the inborn natural tendency of thought to operate implicitly or unconsciously. Reflection is one of the control process in achieving this ideal according to Piaget (1971). For Piaget reflective abstraction is an explicit constructive mental behavior. Important to our thesis is the self as the originator of the process. In contrast to the inborn unconscious thought, reflective abstraction is an explicit act designed to create meaning and understanding.

Thus far we have noted that while autonomous learning may provide the greatest probability for a learner to manifest psychological and pedagogical control, pedagogical self-directed learning settings are the kinds of situations we are discussing here. Furthermore, we have noted that psychological control is both necessary and sufficient for an activity to be described as self-directed learning. Also we have observed that the idea of psychological control is reflected, somewhat imperfectly, but acceptably by Garrison's concept of control and Rich's idea of freedom to. Yet, in our zeal and interest in self-directed learning we have placed primary emphasis on pedagogical aspects of self-directed learning, while generally neglecting the psychological element. This condition may explain why many educational courses designed with pedagogical self-directed learning goals in mind have met with opposition and dissatisfaction. Following Rich's (1986) ideas we may be guilty of providing "freedom from" rather than "freedom to." Or we may have provided independence for students who were not sufficiently proficient either psychologically or in terms of content to address the learning goals.

The discussion of self-directed learning may often conjure up the image of isolated teacherless individual learners. The image is not without merit, but as teachers we have limited contact with these learners. In contrast we frequently have contact with individuals in group learning situations where we have or can provide great opportunity to engage in pedagogical self-directed learning. Some may even know how to do this fairly well. Yet, we do not have sufficient understanding of the psychological aspects of self-directed learning. The situation is comparable to building a ball park or stadium with no knowledge of the rules of the game that will be played there.

A Proposed Theory
Recently, however, I have developed a theoretical framework that may be helpful, at least to those concerned about self-directed learning, that involves the learner in group activity. Figure 1.1 illustrates the idea.

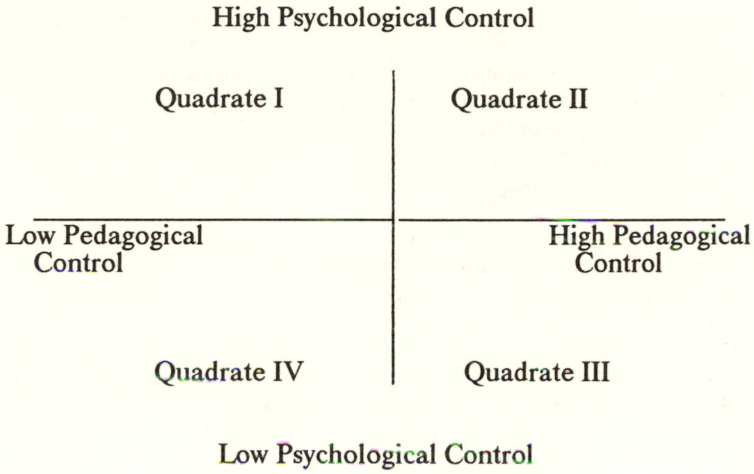

High Psychological Control

| Quadrate I | Quadrate II |

Low Pedagogical
Control   High Pedagogical
                                             Control

| Quadrate IV | Quadrate III |

Low Psychological Control

Figure 1.1: An Illustration of the Relationship Between Pedagogical and Psychological Control in Self-Directed Learning.

Figure 1.1 demonstrates the differing degrees of pedagogical and psychological and influence in self-direction in adult learning. In Quadrate I the learner has high psychological control and the teacher makes use of low pedagogical control techniques. Quadrate II illustrates a condition where high psychological control and high pedagogical control exists. Quadrate III represents a condition characterized by high pedagogical control and low psychological control. Finally Quadrate IV reflects a situation distinguished by low pedagogical and low psychological control.

My theoretical position suggests that self-direction in learning is likely to highest in Quadrate I and lowest in Quadrate III. Perhaps surprisingly, it is suggested that more self-direction in learning will occur in Quadrate II (high pedagogical control - high psychological control) than in its opposite Quadrate IV (low pedagogical control - low psychological control), providing the learner remains in the learning activity. The likelihood of a learner dropping out is probably greatest under the conditions represented by Quadrate II. It is likely that personal learner dissatisfaction will be high in both Quadrates II and IV. Yet, as suggested earlier, the learner with relatively low psychological strength will possibly remain enrolled while expressing dissatisfaction in covert ways. In contrast learner satisfaction will be high in Quadrates I and III. In essence, Quadrates I and III provide a situation where the psychological preference of the learner is matched with a non-threatening pedagogical structure. In Quadrates II and IV a mismatch exists and in both conditions the learner is subject to threat and anxiety. However, in the situation represented by Quadrate II the learner's psychological strength will be an asset, whereas, in Quadrate IV the learner's relatively weak psychological strength will interact negatively with the relative absence of pedagogical structure.

No direct studies have been identified that were specifically designed to test the above theoretical position. Nevertheless, it appears that other theoretical positions, including those discussed earlier in this chapter, have some empirical support consistent with the position I am proposing here.

Summary and Conclusions

This chapter calls attention to some of the emerging issues in theory and practice in adult self-directed learning. It is noted that an increasing number of researchers in adult self-direction in learning are investigating psychological aspects of the phenomenon. It appears that such an approach will contribute much more to effectively designed opportunities for self-directed learning than will concepts limited to learner isolation. The theoretical concept proposed in this chapter contains promise. It does not conflict with important metacognitive theory and it appears to be amenable to empirical testing.

REFERENCES

Atkinson, R. and Shriffren, R. (1968). Human Memory: A proposed system and its control processes. In K.W. Spence and J.T. Spence (Eds.) The psychology of learning and motivation. Vol. 2. New York: Academic Press.

Brookfield, S. (1984). Adult learners, adult education and the community. New York: Teachers College Press.

Brookfield, S. (1985). Self-directed learning: A critical review of research. In S. Brookfield (ed) Self-directed learning: From theory to practice. (New Directions for Continuing Education Series.) San Francisco: Josey-Bass.

Brookfield, S. (1988). Conceptual, methodological and practical ambiguities in self-directed learning. In H. Long and Associates, Self-directed learning: Application and Theory. Athens, Georgia: Adult Education Department, University of Georgia.

Brunner, J. (1971). The relevance of education. New York: Norton.

Gagne', R. (1985). The condition of learning and the theory of instruction (fourth edition). New York: Holt, Rinehart and Winston.

Garrison, R. (in press). Independence and control. In Garrison, R. Understanding distance education: A framework for the future. London: Croom-Helm.

Greeno, J. and Bjork, R. (1973). Mathematical learning theory and the new "mental forestry." Annual Review of Psychology, 24, 81-116.

Kasworm, C. (1988). Self-directed learning in institutional contexts: An exploratory study of adult self-directed learners in higher education. In H. Long & Associates, Self-directed learning: Application & Theory. Athens, Georgia: Adult Education Department, University of Georgia.

Knowles, M. (1975). Self-directed learning: A guide for teachers. Chicago: Association Press.

Long, H. (1986). Self-direction in learning: Conceptual difficulties. Lifelong Learning Forum, 3 (1).pp 1-2.

Long, H. (1988). Self-directed learning reconsidered. In H. Long and Associates, Self-directed learning: Application & Theory. Athens, Georgia: Adult Education Department, University of Georgia.

Piaget, J. (1970). Genetic epistemology. New York: W.W. Horton.

Piaget, J. (1971). Biology and Knowledge. Chicago: The University of Chicago Press.

Piaget, J. (1972). Judgement and Reasoning in the Child. Otawa: Littlefield, Adams and Co.

Rich, J. (1986). Student freedom in the classroom. The Journal of Educational Thought, 20, (3), pp. 125-133.

Rothkoph, E. (1970). The concept of mathemagenic activities. Review of Educational Research, 40, 325-336.

Skinner, B. (1968). The technology of teaching. New York: Appleton.

Tough, A. (1967). Learning without a teacher. Educational Research Series No. 3. Toronto, Canada: The Ontario Institute for Studies in Education.

Chapter Two

SELF-DIRECTED ORIENTATION TOWARD LEARNING: A LEARNING STYLE?*

L. Adrianne Bonham

The concept of self-directed learning in adult education has changed over the years. Self-directed learning has been conceived as a characteristic of all adult learners and as a goal toward which adult learners should be moved, as an instructional method used naturally by adults and as one which should be taught to them, as the use of instructional design principles for planning one's own learning and as a process in which the learner moves from one learning episode to the next in an order governed by availability of resources. The readiness to do self-directed learning has also been defined as a trait which individuals possess to varying degrees; this recent theory development has opened the way to consider whether self-directed orientation toward learning (SDOL) may be a learning style. This paper reviews literature bearing on this question and proposes possible constructs of self-directedness as learning style.

The literature is reviewed in relation to three conceptual areas: definitions of learning style, definitions of self-directed learning, and existing instruments for measuring SDOL. These sections are followed by an attempt to define perspectives still missing if SDOL is to be conceived and measured as a learning style. The final section offers a tentative model for a set of learning styles oriented around the degree and kind of self-directedness in learning.

DEFINITIONS OF LEARNING STYLE

Two kinds of definitions exist for learning styles; broadly stated ones and others that define specific elements. A typical broad definition is, "a student's consistent way of

---

*A similar line of reasoning--and limited portions of the text--of this paper were originally presented in Bonham (1987). Bonham is assistant professor of adult and continuing education in the Department of Interdisciplinary Education, College of Education, Texas A&M Univ., College Station, TX.

responding and using stimuli in the context of learning" (Claxton & Ralston, 1978, p. 1). Problems exist, not with such broad definitions, but only when researchers begin to define the style alternatives or elements. Some suggest only cognitive elements (e.g., Kolb, 1976); others suggest various affective and physiological elements (e.g., Keefe, 1979). While some theorists propose classification schemes for the elements, it seems that there is little or no agreement about a comprehensive definition that would determine or justify the list of elements. For present purposes, a learning style will be thought of as a way of acting or thinking in a learning situation; the person feels comfortable with that approach and possesses any skills necessary for using it; when there is a choice, the person habitually chooses this approach. A corollary is that this style contrasts with one or more equally well-defined styles delineated by an encompassing theory. (For brevity in this paper, the various styles will be called opposites, even though they may not be true opposites if there is a plurality of styles.) Each style is most useful in some setting but can be dysfunctional if used all the time.

At the least, the eclectic situation just defined opens the possibility of adding SDOL as another cluster of learning style elements which can fit existing broad definitions of learning style. One might hope that such a cluster would eventually be found to correlate with, or even subsume, some of the style elements arising in other theories.

Three kinds of information support the idea that SDOL is a learning style: evidence that other learning styles include elements relevant to the definition of SDOL; evidence that SDOL is treated as a style by writers; and experimental evidence that shows SDOL acts like a style.

A number of learning style instruments--including Canfield Learning Styles Inventory, Grasha-Riechmann Student Learning Styles Scales, Hill Cognitive Styles Inventory, Productivity Environmental Preference Survey, Renzulli and Smith Learning Styles Inventory, the Rezler and French instrument, and Myers-Briggs Type Indicator--have elements related to independence in the learning situation, which is considered at least an aspect of SDOL (Long, 1985b, 1986b). In proposing models of SDOL, both Guglielmino (1977/1978) and Oddi (1984/1985) identify independence as a component.

While writers have not always labeled SDOL a learning style, they have sometimes described it in similar terms. Hiemstra (1985), in a review of research on the learning projects of older adults, identified SDOL and cognitive/learning styles as elements deserving further research--and even asked how they might interact--but did not call SDOL a style dimension. Penland (1979), finding the existence of self-planned learning to be even more uniformly distributed in the population than had previously been thought, identified two reasons for choosing self-direction: the desires to learn at one's own pace and in one's own style. Yet, he did not identify SDOL as a style. Although identifying demographics that characterize self-directed learners, Tough (1978) still said, "The really large differences are within any given population, not between populations" (p. 252). He did not say that differences might be caused by stylistic dimensions within individuals.

Periodically, researchers have made statements that cast SDOL as a learning style. Some statements identify the polarity that sometimes characterizes a style.

> Educators are challenged to distinguish between those adults who possess the characteristics often believed to be associated with self-direction in learning and those adults who fail to reveal such attributes (Long & Agyekum, 1983, p. 77).

Long (1986a) acknowledged the question of whether SDOL is a cognitive orientation or style. Caffarella and O'Donnell (1988) suggested that it would be helpful to view SDOL as a personality construct instead of just as a mode of instruction, and that learning styles should be examined in determining how individuals conduct self-directed learning. Hiemstra (1988) indicated his belief that some persons have self-directing tendencies or readinesses while others do not. Even (1978) equated SDOL with field independence and called it either a cognitive style or a cognitive strategy (learned and deliberately chosen). Merriam (1986) said self-directed learning could be classified with other cognitive styles. Brookfield (1988) called self-directed learning an adult learning style; it is uncertain, however, that he meant anything more than that it is an adult approach to learning.

As further evidence that SDOL is treated like a style, Caffarella and Caffarella (1986) distinguished between readiness for self-directed learning and competencies for self-directed learning, thus seemingly contrasting a style dimension with an ability dimension. They said, further, "The instrument may only be measuring attitudes toward self-directedness versus any specific abilities or skills a person might have in carrying out learning activities in a self-directed manner" (p. 232).

In terms of experimental evidence, Caffarella and Caffarella (1986) found that use of learning contracts had little impact on SDOL but did have some impact on competencies. Furthermore, the differences were found despite the fact that both constructs were measured by self-report instruments and subjects might have tended to rate themselves alike on the two. This is the result that might be expected from a not-easily-modified style interacting with the need for certain skills, that are more easily learned.

Kasworm (1983-84) taught a graduate course in which both method and content were self-directed learning, hypothesizing that the course would increase SDLRS scores. Gain/loss scores, however, showed wide differences that could not be accounted for by such obvious moderator variables as student status, age, academic major, or previous experience with self-directed learning. One-fourth of the students reacted negatively to the idea of self-directed learning in graduate courses--even after completing the course. Only 40% made a shift in the conceptual level at which they operated, indicating that learning had not been thoroughly internalized by a majority of the students. It seems worth considering that the uneven responses might reflect style-like differences in SDOL.

Bowes and Smith (1986) tried to train adult basic education instructors in self-directed learning but also got an uneven response, raising "the question of how adequately we can predict how people will respond to self-directed learning" (p. 9). They did find that persons who scored at or above 60% on the SDLRS "encountered little or no difficulty in conceptualizing, planning, conducting, and evaluating their own project" (p. 10). Because the training should have provided necessary skills, it is possible that remaining differences were the result of style preferences.

Spear and Mocker (1984) identified the relevant concept in self-directed learning as the Organizing Circumstance. "Circumstance is defined as a subjective concept which gives meaning to the individual's environment" (p. 4). These researchers chose to focus on the environment's effect as the learner encounters resources for learning. A focus on the learner's subjective response, however, could produce a style-like concept. Such a concept might explain why one learner habitually encounters a book, for instance, while another habitually encounters persons who can assist in learning. In fact, this concept might help to explain why some people are sensitive to multiple naturally occurring resources and others are sensitive chiefly or only to contrived resources like classes, programmed instruction, and learning contracts.

Spear's (1988) search for a methodology for the study of self-directed learning may offer an idea related to SDOL as a learning style. He theorized that self-directed learning must be understood in terms of nonlinear clusters of events instead of in terms of the linear planning of curriculum design. Rather than selecting resources by evaluation and logic, the learner uses the resource at hand, without knowing exactly how it fits into a broad plan or how it will ultimately contribute to the learning goal. Eventually, the learner synthesizes knowledge gained in the distinct clusters. Spear (1988) raises the question of whether there are "particular attributes or talents that make some people more facile than others when engaged in self-directed learning projects" (p. 217). This question seems especially appropriate because the reciprocal-determinism model he uses for theory building hypothesizes an interaction of environment, overt behavior, and cognitive-personal factors (which this reader feels might also be called learning style). The question also seems appropriate because of Spear's (1988) emphasis on the subjective nature of the Organizing Circumstance. This line of speculation is continued later in the paper.

The strongest evidence that SDOL is seen as a learning style comes in the relatively recent work on instruments to measure degree of potential self-directedness in learning. Guglielmino (1977/1978) and Oddi (1984/1985, 1986) both assume that SDOL is a relatively stable characteristic on which people vary and which affects the ways people learn or prefer to learn. Thus, it sounds as if they are defining learning styles. Their two instruments are discussed later in this paper.

DEFINITIONS OF SELF-DIRECTED LEARNING

When one reviews the body of literature on self-directed learning, it becomes evident that researchers use the same term to refer to a variety of activities. It would be difficult to discuss potential learning styles without first deciding on a meaning for self-directed learning--or at least deciding on a model for relating multiple definitions. This section presents a scheme for relating multiple definitions and shows that it is impractical to attempt a definition that would be so broad as to include all instances in which the term has been used. The scheme is shown in Table 2.1.

For present purposes, learning may be said to take place in two kinds of settings: educational and non-educational. Within the educational setting, a situation may be teacher-oriented (the teacher is chiefly responsible for planning the educational experience--column A of Table 1) or learner-oriented (the learner is expected to have major input in planning the educational experience--column B). In the non-educational setting, there are potentially three ways in which learning may take place: The learner may plan learning in the same way it is planned in an educational setting (column C); the learner may plan learning in a more holistic, non-linear fashion (column D); and the learner may learn incidentally or without any intention to learn (column E). To the non-educational setting is added a final category, non-learning, in which neither intended nor incidental learning occurs (column F).

In studying self-directed learning, researchers have usually focused on one or more aspects of the learning situation: motivation (row 1 of Table 1); choice of content to be learned, goals, methods, and resources (row 2); choice of time and place for learning (row 3); and sequencing of goals, methods, resources, time, and place (row 4). Time and place are identified separately from content, goals, methods, and resources only becuase of the examples given below.

Table 2.1. A Model for Positioning Theories and Research
Studies in Terms of Their Definition of Self-Directed
Learning goals, methods, resources, time, and place (row 4). Time
and place are identified separately from content, goals, methods, and
resources only because of the examples given below.

SETTINGS
EDUCATIONAL   NON-EDUCATIONAL

Teacher-Oriented (A)	Learner-Oriented (B)	Instruction-Oriented (C)	Deliberate Learning In Non-Instructional Format (D)	Incidental Learning (E)	Non-Learning (F)

COMPONENTS

Motivation (1)
1A	1B	1C	1D	1E	1F

Content, Goals, Methods, Resources, Evaluation (2)
2A	2B	2C	2D	2E	2F

Time and Place (3)
3A	3B	3C	3D	3E	3F

Sequencing (4)
4A	4B	4C	4D	4E	4F

The knowledgeable reader of self-directed learning literature
may question the exclusion of Brookfield's (1986) change of
consciousness from this model. This reader feels it is best omitted
here because all other theories deal with the circumstances of
learning. Brookfield's view is incorporated in the definitions of
possible learning styles given later.

Some examples show how the meanings of studies change,
based on which cells are relevant in Table 1. Occasionally,
researchers are primarily concerned with the motivation of students to
assume responsibility, even if that means responsibility in carrying out
plans made by a teacher (as seems to be the idea held by Kasworm's
[1988] subjects); self-directedness thus falls into cell 1B and is
contrasted with other-directedness of motivation (cell 1A). While this
definition is not often stated by researchers, this writer believes it is
one often assumed by lay persons _and_ by researchers.

When self-directed learning is equated with independent study (DeRoos, 1982) or correspondence courses (Carpenter, 1981), self-directedness is found in cell 3C and contrasts with cells 3A and 3B. Not so obvious is the fact that such study also involves cells 2 and 4 in column A; the teacher/ planner is in control of content, goals, methods, and resources--and the way in which these are sequenced in the course. The learner controls only when and where to study.

Using self-directed learning as an instructional method (e.g., Caffarella & Caffarella, 1986; Knowles, 1975; Reed, 1980; Savoie, 1979; Wiley, 1981) creates a complex pattern. The teacher chooses self-directed learning as the broad method (cell 2A) and expects the learner to choose content and goals (2B) within the scope of the class (which the teacher or institution sets, 2A). The learner is also expected to choose specific methods and resources (2B) and to plan the sequencing of components (4B), so as to finish within prescribed time limits for the course (3A). The teacher's intention in such planning seems to be helping the learner develop planning skills to use outside the classroom (column C), assuming that such learning is planned in the same way that the teacher plans a class.

That assumption is consistent with ones made by Tough (1971) and others who use his interview protocol (e.g., Cobb, 1978; Geisler, 1984; Peters & Gordon, 1974; Rymell & Newsom, 1981) or a model similar to his (Bowes & Smith, 1986). Self-directed learning in everyday life is conceived to be a structured experience in which the learner plans and conducts learning as if it were an instructional process. The learner provides his/her own motivation (cell 1C), as well as planning aspects of the learning process (2C-4C). The term "self-instruction" might well be applied to this model (Penland, 1981). Sometimes the opposite of this kind of self-directedness seems to be anything that occurs in an educational setting (columns A or B) (Bowes & Smith, 1986; Gibbons et al., 1980; Gross, Tough, & Hebert, 1979; Kathrein, 1981; Mocker & Spear, 1982). At other times, when educational experiences are described as part of a larger plan conceived by the self-directed learner (e.g., Hiemstra, 1976), the opposite of self-directedness seems to be non-learning (column F).

An alternate model of self-directed learning in everyday life (column D) rejects the idea of detailed planning of a linear process in favor of a holistic, nonlinear process that is planned as learning progresses. The strongest contrast between the instructional model (column C) and the inquiry model (column D) is in how sequencing (row 4) is conceived. The instructional model assumes that goals are already defined, that detailed planning is done at the beginning of a learning project, and that each activity is chosen for its perceived effectiveness in meeting goals (cell 4C); allowance is made for changing plans as learning progresses and the learner discovers new resources or restructures the knowledge being gained (Penland, 1981). The inquiry model emphasizes that the learner begins with a general need to know, finds resources as they become available or come to attention, does most planning as the learning is in progress, and does not know initially how useful a given resources or piece of information may become (cell 4D). In terms of sequencing, emphasis is on methods and resources (2D) that are available (Danis & Tremblay, 1988; Spear, 1988; Spear & Mocker, 1984). There does not seem to be a single pattern opposite to this inquiry one; this model (column D) seems to contrast with columns A, B, and C.

According to the Spear and Mocker (1984; Spear, 1988) model, the line is not always clear between deliberate (column D) and incidental (column E) learning. Fortuitous action and fortuitous environment represent elements of chance or near-chance in Spear's (1988) categories for classifying elements in data analysis. The factor that puts even these actions and environmental effects into the category of deliberate learning is the incorporation of incidental learning into a broader context of some deliberate learning.

Surprisingly, it is unclear where to locate on Table 1 the two instruments--Guglielmino's SDLRS and the ODDI Continuing Learning Inventory--used most often to measure SDOL. Reasons for this statement are explored in the next section.

For present purposes, it is suggested that certain definitions of self-directed learning not be considered, because they deal only with one component in learning (e.g., correspondence courses and independent study are self-directed only in terms of time and place--row 3). Motivation (row 1) by itself seems a misleading definition, because there can be motivation to learn without motivation to take responsibility for planning learning. On the other hand, as shown later, motivation can be seen as a component in all SDOL styles. Non-learning should be eliminated from consideration as a condition opposite to self-directedness, for reasons explained later. The remaining definition of self-directed learning distinguishes between other-directed learning and self-directed learning, between self-directed learning in a class and outside a class, and between instruction-oriented and inquiry-oriented self-directed learning outside of a class.

EXISTING INSTRUMENTS

Two instruments measuring SDOL are prominently referenced in adult education literature. They are discussed here in terms of their underlying theories, their psychometric properties, and their possible use as measures of SDOL as a learning style.

Self-Directed Learning Readiness Scale
Lucy Guglielmino (1977/1978) devised the SDLRS in 1977 as a way to measure individuals' likelihood of doing self-directed learning, conceived according to Tough's (1971) instructional model. She had a panel of experts use a modified Delphi technique to define characteristics of a self-directed learner, providing for them this definition of self-direction in learning.

Self-direction in learning can occur in a wide variety of situations, ranging from a teacher-directed classroom to self-planned and self-conducted learning projects. Although certain learning situations are more conducive to self-direction in learning than are others, it is the personal characteristics of the learner--including his attitudes, his values, and his abilities--which ultimately determine whether self-directed learning will take place in a given learning situation. The self-directed learner more often chooses or influences the learning objectives, activities, resources, priorities, and levels of energy expenditure than does the other-directed learner (Guglielmino, 1977/1978, p. 34).

With the experts' responses, Guglielmino constructed items and identified eight factors by factor analysis: openness to learning opportunities, self-concept as an effective learner, initiative and independence in learning, informed acceptance of responsibility for one's own learning, love of learning, creativity, future orientation, and ability to use basic study and problem solving skills (Guglielmino, 1977/1978).

As a result of the factor analysis, Guglielmino (1977/ 1978) provided this definition of a self-directed learner, noting that, while persistence did not emerge as a factor, it permeated other factors.

A highly self-directed learner, based on the survey results, is one who exhibits initiative, independence, and persistence in learning; one who accepts responsibility for his or her own learning and views problems as challenges, not obstacles; one who is capable of self-discipline and has a high degree of curiosity; one who has a strong desire to learn or change and is self-confident; one who is able to use basic study skills, organize his or her time and set an appropriate pace for learning, and to develop a plan for completing work; one who enjoys learning and has a tendency to be goal-oriented (p. 73).

The outcome of Guglielmino's work was an instrument that can be used by educational institutions or individual learning facilitators in their efforts to select suitable learners for programs requiring self-direction in learning and to screen learners to determine their strengths and weaknesses in self-direction in learning in an attempt to guide them into situations in which they can best utilize and develop their potential in this area (Guglielmino, 1977/1978, p. 29).

It should be helpful to compare Guglielmino's statements with Table 2.1. By relating her work to Tough's and describing the need for skill in planning, she places her model in column C. She also says, however, that self-directed learning can occur in a teacher-directed classroom (column A), and that it is even more likely to occur in a classroom where the learner has more initiative (column B). Her statement of purpose for the instrument makes it sound more appropriate for column B than C. While she expects learner control over goals, methods, time, place, and sequencing of these (rows 2-4 of columns B or C), strongest emphasis is on motivation (1B or 1C). The motivation emphasis is so strong, in fact, that one would not be surprised if a learner were called self-directed merely because the person took part enthusiastically in activities planned by the teacher.

To further emphasize the dilemma at hand, one can speculate about what would be the opposite of self-directed learning, according to Guglielmino's model. She identifies the opposite as being other-directed, even while saying self-direction can happen in a teacher-directed classroom. For this reader, there is the strong impression that the true opposite lurking in the background is the non-learner (column F): the one who exhibits no initiative, independence, or persistence in learning; who views problems as obstacles; who lacks curiosity, enjoyment of learning, a strong desire to learn or change, and basic study skills. Discussion will return to this point of opposites as the psychometric properties of the SDLRS are examined.

Every instrument engenders criticism, and the purpose of this paper is not to test the worth of the SDLRS in any general sense. It may be helpful, however, to look at criticisms that may help either to locate the SDLRS in terms of Table 1 or to conceptualize SDOL as a learning style. The SDLRS has been criticized for heavy use of items dealing with reading and classes (Brockett, 1983, 1985), a situation that makes the model seem more appropriate for column A or B than for C. Furthermore, many items deal with learning in general ("I love to learn.") and not with self-directed learning as opposed to other-directed learning. SDLRS score is generally thought to increase with education (Brockett, 1983, 1985; Hassan, 1982; Long & Agyekum, 1983, 1984; Sabbaghian, 1980), which would not necessarily be true if the model belonged in columns C or D.

In summary, the SDLRS seems to measure a propensity for learning in general and not specifically for self-directed learning. If anything, it leans toward learner-oriented activity in an educational environment and not toward the non-educational setting which Tough (1971) envisioned for most of adult learning. It provides no measure of the preference for inquiry learning described for column D of Table 2.1, and it assumes non-learning to be the opposite of what it measures.

Oddi Continuing Learning Inventory

Loris Oddi criticized Guglielmino's theory base because it focused on instructional learning and did not allow for inquiry or performance modes of learning. Wanting to identify persons who would engage in the continuing learning necessary for the practice of a profession, she was interested in "the personality characteristics of individuals whose learning behavior is characterized by initiative and persistence in learning over time through a variety of modes" (Oddi, 1986, p. 98). She read the self-directed learning literature to find personality traits that characterize the self-directed learner and grouped those traits into three overlapping dimensions: Proactive Drive versus Reactive Drive (PD/RD), Cognitive Openness versus Defensiveness (CO/D), and Commitment to Learning versus Apathy or Aversion to Learning

(CL/AAL). She envisioned a continuum between each set of poles, with the first-named trait of each pair being predominant in the self-directed individual.

The salient characteristics of PD/RD consisted of self-regulating behavior, possession of high self-esteem and self-confidence, and engagement in self-initiated and self-sustained learning activity directed toward higher level goals. At the opposite pole of this dimension were the reliance of the individual on extrinsic forces to stimulate learning, a tendency to discontinue activity on encountering obstacles, engagement in learning to meet lower order needs, and low self-confidence. . . .

Salient characteristics of CO/D included openness to new ideas and activities, ability to adapt to change, and tolerance of ambiguity. The opposite pole included attributes such as rigidity, fear of failure, and avoidance of new ideas and activities. . . .

Salient characteristics of CL/AAL included the expression of positive attitudes toward engaging in learning activities of varying sorts and a preference for more thought-provoking leisure pursuits. The opposite pole included expressions of indifference or hostile attitudes toward engaging in learning activities and reports of less engagement in activities commonly regarded as promoting learning (Oddi, 1986, p. 99).

The original conceptualization of the OCLI seems much like the SDLRS in three regards: Its positive dimensions seem to refer to all intentional learning (columns A-D of Table 1), and its negative dimensions seem to refer to non-learning (column F). As with the SDLRS, there is a strong emphasis on motivation. A further problem is that factor analyses in several developmental studies failed to confirm the three hypothesized dimensions, despite the fact that Oddi reworked items for the purpose of obtaining those dimensions. In the OCLI's present form, three factors are found: a general and predominant factor for self-confidence, ability to work independently, and preference for learning with others; and two lesser factors, for reading avidity and ability to be self-regulating. Oddi's (1984/1985, 1986) descriptions of the self-directed continuing learner seem to point toward general psychological adjustment, as do the hypothesized and obtained factors.

For the sake of clarity, it is also important to note that Oddi's references to the inquiry mode are based on Houle's (1961) work and not on the later work of Spear and Mocker (1984; Spear, 1988). Thus, the OCLI makes no attempt to reflect Organizing Circumstances or other aspects of the model associated with column D of Table 2.1.

Conclusions. The SDLRS and OCLI seem designed to discover the person who likes to learn in any setting. That function is consistent with the original purposes of the instrument designers and seems, to this reviewer, a useful function. By intention, however, the instruments do little to distinguish--among avid learners--those who prefer self-directedness and those who prefer something else.

Perhaps this fact explains the lack of supporting data when researchers try to increase SDLRS scores by teaching skills for self-directed learning. The treatments are designed to increase self-directedness as opposed to other-directedness (Caffarella & Caffarella, 1986; Kasworm, 1983-1984), while the instrument is measuring love of learning as opposed to non-learning.

Both instruments present an additional problem if SDOL is to be characterized as a learning style. Most advocates of style theories view each style as useful in an appropriate context, but theories behind the SDLRS and OCLI assume that self-directedness (avidity for learning) is positive and its opposite (non-learning) is negative. This problem becomes a basis for further theory development in the next section.

MISSING ELEMENTS

There seem to be five closely related things lacking if SDOL is to be thought of--and measured--as a learning style. Opposites must be as clearly defined as the beginning concepts are. Distinction must be made between self-directed learning and other kinds of learning (not between learning and non-learning). Distinction must also be made among different kinds of self-directedness in learning. There must be a greater awareness of the potential usefulness of various styles, rather than rating one style positively and its opposite negatively. Finally, preference for certain methods and resources must be measured as a possible influence on how persons conduct self-directed learning.

Defining Opposites

Theory building for the SDLRS seems particularly lacking in definition of what self-directedness is not. While the opposite in individual dimensions is well-defined for the OCLI, less attention seems to be given to defining the non-self-directed continuing learner. Evidence of such lack of definition is research, previously noted, that seems to misuse an instrument. Certainly, when defining learning style elements, it is necessary to do an equally thorough job of defining each; and when developing an instrument, it is necessary to measure each element directly, instead of assuming that presence of one element means absence of another.

Distinguishing Self-Directedness From Other Kinds of Learning

The SDLRS and OCLI distinguish between motivation (resulting in learning) and lack of motivation (resulting in non-learning). What is needed is a distinction between self-directed learning and some other kind(s) of learning. The logical alternative is other-directed learning, whether the direction is provided by a teacher, book, videotape, or some other resource that provides both content and process guidance.

Distinguishing Different Kinds of Self-Directedness in Learning

No instruments exist that distinguish between self-directedness in a class setting and outside of one, or between instructional and inquiry modes of learning. Those differences might be among different styles, or there may be different settings (educational and non-educational) in which one or more styles are exhibited.

Defining Positively Valued Styles

A strength of the broad concept of learning styles is that it attaches positive value to different ways of learning. Individual learning style theories most often do this by asserting that one style is most useful in one situation while another is most useful in another situation. While this criterion of positively valued elements is necessary for considering SDOL to be a learning style, it also seems realistic and useful for the purposes of adult education in general. This assertion is explored further in the section of the paper that defines potential styles.

Distinguishing Among Preferred Methods and Resources

The SDLRS has been criticized for its emphasis on reading and classes as methods or resources for learning. One of the OCLI factors is avidity for reading. Critics of these instruments (and of self-directed learning theory generally) have criticized the lack of attention to other persons as resources for learning (e.g., Brookfield, 1986). Furthermore, the instrument developers' choice to overemphasize schooling-type methods/resources may explain why scores seem so closely tied to level of education.

The assertion of Spear and Mocker (1984) is that ready availability of a given resource is what determines its use. This writer wants to add the possibility that differential sensitivity to available resources may be a style-like quality in individuals. Some learners may habitually see the books in their environment, for instance, while others see the live experts. (Danis and Tremblay's [1988] findings must also be dealt with, however. They found that self-taught learners used a variety of methods [implying that learners do not habitually choose the same ones] and that these learners consulted experts only after they knew something about the field of study [a choice related to learning progress and not to personal preference].)

The issue of whether to measure resource/method preferences, however, is separate from the issue of whether they exist. This writer feels an instrument would be useful if it only measured the kinds of learning preferred (other-directed, instructionally self-directed in a class, instructionally self-directed outside of a class, self-directed in an inquiry mode in or outside of a class) and did not also try to identify preferred resources or methods.

The latter task might be accomplished by a separate instrument. This approach would be especially helpful because it would allow identification of preferred methods and resources, regardless of whether the person is other- or self-directed.

A PROPOSED MODEL FOR A LEARNING STYLE CONSTRUCT

To this point, a line of reasoning has been proposed that goes beyond existing empirical evidence at several points. Any model proposed for SDOL learning styles, therefore, is tentative--almost an example of what might be. For that reason, Tables 2.2 and 2.3 present general descriptions of how the styles might be exhibited in educational and non-educational settings, and what the value of each style might be in each setting. Those tables also describe a non-learner, for the sake of comparison. Table 2.4 gives a more extensive description of styles that might actually be measured by an instrument. Finally, questions are raised.

Ideas related to the inquiry mode were inspired by the work of Spear and Mocker (1984; Spear, 1988) and Danis and Tremblay (1988). Ideas related to the instructional mode were drawn from a number of sources using the orientation established by Tough (1971). In defining possible styles, the approach was to take statements describing the learning and interpret them as characteristics or preferences of persons who learn in that way. Emphasis is on contrast among the styles, rather than on ways they are alike.

The Model

Three styles are proposed: other-directed, self-directed in the instructional mode, and self-directed in the inquiry mode. Possible characteristics of each style are given in Table 2:4. An instrument devised to measure these styles should include items about classroom and non-classroom learning, and early studies should seek to determine whether the two settings represent separate styles (making a total of six styles). Through factor analysis, for instance, it might be determined that some persons prefer to perform in the instructional mode in a class but in the inquiry mode outside of a class.

The other-directed learner, although motivated to learn, prefers to have the teacher define and organize content and learning approaches, and shows panic or hostility if expected to make such decisions without considerable guidance. Outside the classroom, this person chooses resources that provide their own plans for how material will be learned. In any setting, this learner will understand concepts if they are presented but may not think to connect information if pieces are given in isolation. While being other-directed is often viewed negatively by educators, it does prove to be a useful approach in some cases: when the learner knows almost nothing about a new field of study, when some clearly defined content must be learned quickly, when the goal is training rather than education, or when a learner has no choice but to follow plans made by someone else (e.g., when a correspondence course must be completed). Other-directedness is a weak approach when no teacher or resource is available to guide learning and when new knowledge must be created.

A desire to be well organized is an outstanding characteristic of the person who is self-directed according to the instructional model. Such a learner emphasizes linearity in thinking, outlines papers well, and habitually does detailed planning. This person often has a high level of formal education, because he/she likes the structure required in a classroom but is also willing to participate--in fact, insists on participating--in planning the learning. When this person plans learning, it is usually done in small, discrete projects linked in an orderly manner. When the learner chooses among available learning methods and resources, choice is strongly influenced by perceived effectiveness of that approach. This style is most effective when the teacher must be satisfied as to the quality of the student's planning, when the learner already knows something about the topic, and when the chief task is finding existing knowledge (as opposed to creating new knowledge). The person who habitually uses this style may have problems when teachers do not allow individual planning, when a plan is thwarted (by lack of resources, for instance), or when new knowledge must be synthesized.

The person who is self-directed according to the inquiry model thinks holistically and tends not to do detailed planning at the beginning of any project. Even if structure is provided for content, this person must think through and understand the structure before accepting it or revising it. This learner has particular sensitivity to things or people in the environment that can be learning resources, and uses those resources whenever they are encountered (even if it is not immediately clear how the information is relevant). When there is a choice among available resources, choice is made on the basis of feelings about the activity, more than because of a reasoned judgment about the effectiveness of the resource. This person is willing to live with any frustration created by receiving information piecemeal and having to organize it for himself/herself. There is less tendency to identify separate learning projects and more tendency to see all learning as one ongoing activity. This approach is most effective when new knowledge must be created, especially if it must be drawn from a broad and poorly defined field of knowledge. It may also be best when the use of the newly acquired information requires a solid understanding of underlying principles that organize the body of knowledge; teaching the information is one such use. To the chagrin of a teacher, this learner may not do well--and may show hostility--if forced to lay out a detailed learning plan in advance.

Does anyone learn by the self-directed instructional model? Is the instructional mode of self-directed learning used by anyone, or is it an artifact of early research designs? Subsequent research may show that

Table 2:2. Styles Exhibited in Education Settings.

Non-Learner	Other-Directed Learner	Self-Directed Instructional Model	Self-Directed Inquiry Model
		Description	
Usually not present because of voluntary nature of adult education; if attendance is forced, exhibits indifference or hostility. This state is not a style but blocks emergence of whatever style the learner might otherwise have.	Participates enthusiastically as teacher leads; depends on teacher to provide structure for content and educational planning. Exhibits panic or hostility if teacher expects learners to do educational planning or interpret and reshape content. Learns content whether it is logically organized or not, but does not do well at organizing material when it is presented without a framework.	Has own ideas of what to learn and how to learn it; plans in detailed ways. If teacher does not expect learners to plan, this learner does so anyway and may have well-defined conflict with teacher's plans. If teacher expects planning, does it thoroughly and carries out plan. Experiences frustration if classroom activities are not clearly goal-oriented or do not present content with logical progression.	Has own ideas of what to learn but may be less sure of exact goals or how to achieve them. If teacher does not expect learner planning, will follow teacher's lead but enrich learning with seemingly unplanned additions; in the course of pursuing these leads, may cease to follow teacher's lead. Even if content framework is provided, may need to think through it as if framework did not exist and come up with own framework. If teacher expects learner planning (by instructional model), experiences frustration in clearly defining goals; resists laying out a plan of learning, preferring to make it up while in the process of learning.

Table 2:2 con't. Styles Exhibited in Educational Settings

Motivation	When Style Is of Value
Motivated to learn and to explore where interests lead; motivation is enhanced by context that encourages exploration and does not demand that learner produce a structured plan or only follow the teacher's plan.	Most useful when teacher provides some structure but also encourages exploration, when learning content must be drawn from a broad and poorly defined scope, when a new synthesis or new content must be created.
Motivated to learn and to plan for learning; motivation is enhanced by context that encourages structured planning by the learner.	Most useful when teacher expects learners to plan own learning, when the learning content is narrowly defined, when desired content has already been synthesized to some degree by existing resources.
Motivated to learn; motivation is enhanced by presence of structure.	Most useful style when teacher expects to direct learning, when learner knows little about the subject, when learner lacks some of the skills required by other styles, or when the learning goal is in the area of training rather than education.
Either unmotivated by a classroom atmosphere or negatively motivated (motivated to disrupt the class prevent own participation).	Not ever an effective state; change in motivation allows for emergence of a useful style.

29

Table 2:3. Styles Exhibited Outside of Educational Settings

Non-Learner	Other-Directed Learner	Self-Directed Instructional Model	Self-Directed Inquiry Model
		Description	
Does not seek out learning opportunities; does not see learning potential in daily events. Does not view learning as a way to solve problems; tends not to apply existing knowledge to new problems.	Chooses a book, videotape, etc., that provides both structure and content for learning. Seeks people who will guide in how and what to learn. Tends to use one resource per need. Learning is in isolated episodes that are usually triggered by outside events. Learning is utilitarian.	Thinks through a learning need until it is fairly well defined; may gather information about resources before laying out a plan of action. Uses multiple resources efficiently for a given problem, but tends to define problems narrowly. Learning episodes are clearly differentiated from one another (even when they deal with the same broad subject) but are frequent. Learning is utilitarian but enjoyable when learner is able to devise a clear plan.	Begins a learning project before a goal is clearly defined. Likes freedom to explore; is not frustrated by deadends or uncertainty about how information fits the need. Efficiency is not a chief concern. Uses multiple resources but may tend to choose them for their accessibility or for the pleasure of the learning activity rather than for optimum relevance. Tends to have broad on going learning projects in which episodes are not clearly differentiated. While a use can be stated for the learning, primary motivation may be the pleasure of learning or of using the skill being learned. Does not distinguish sharply between learning and other activities.

Table 2:3 con't. Styles Exhibited Outside of Educational Settings

	Motivation	When Style Is of Value
Unmotivated to learn; does not see everyday events for their learning potential.	Not ever an effective state; change in motivation allows for emergence of a useful styles.	
Motivated to learn if recognize a specific need; motivated to seek out resources that will structure learning.	Most useful when there is a simple, well-defined need for which a resource resists; when the learning goal is in an area of training rather than education; when the goal must be met quickly.	
Motivated to learn and to plan for learning. Likes sense of control when can plan in detail	Most useful when the goal can be clearly defined, when it can be met with only a few resources, when desired content has already been synthesized to some degree by existing resources, when efficiency of time and effort is beneficial, when all resources are available on demand.	
Motivated to learn for utilitarian reasons but, more often, for pleasure of learning or of using the skill being learned.	Most useful when goals can be defined only broadly at first, when the scope of the content is broad, when a new synthesis or new content must be created, when the pleasurable process of learning is as important as meeting a goal, when there is sufficient time to do things inefficiently, when outside factors govern when resources become available	

people do not do extensive preplanning but that they remember their experiences as being more deliberate and linear than was actually the case; persons with higher levels of formal education might be even more likely than less educated persons to describe their learning in these terms. Some form of the inquiry model may come to dominate the field of self-directed learning research, as a step beyond the assumptions made by earlier researchers. At this point, however, it seems best to retain the possibility of a style that emphasizes preplanning. Perhaps the best way to test whether such an approach to learning does exist is to see whether anyone has a style that emphasizes planning at the beginning of a project.

Where does Brookfield's concept of self-directed learning fit into a style scheme? Brookfield's (1984, 1986) concept is omitted deliberately from the model (Table 1) for relating definitions of self-directed learning. The omission is based on the fact that he is concerned, not with how learning is planned, but with the internal change of consciousness that he says should result. It seems that such change can take place regardless of who plans learning or whether planning is done before or during learning. Change of consciousness can take place in a group or when a learner confronts a body of knowledge alone. Two points seem relevant to the model proposed here. First, the learner may consider restructuring knowledge but deliberately choose to value and retain existing meanings; even in such a case, there is a change of consciousness because the person has recognized that there is a choice. Second, while persons with any of the styles may experience a change of consciousness about content, the other-directed learner would seem least likely to do so; the person who chooses to be led in planning for learning is likely to be led in accepting the meaning given by the teacher or text. Perhaps the person who is self-directed by the inquiry model is most likely to experience a change of consciousness, because no prior structure is imposed on the learning process.

Is it possible that there are other styles in the SDOL cluster? At this stage, it would be premature to rule out the possibility of other styles. In particular, it is necessary to consider Brookfield's (1988) emphasis on collaborative learning. The desire to learn with others is different from the desire to learn from others (to be other-directed). Neither is it the same as the self-directed learner's preference for using other persons--rather than books, for instance--as resources for the content to be learned. Further thought on the characteristics of the collaborative learner might open the way to defining a style-like preference for this approach, in educational and/or non-educational settings. It would contrast with two styles in the present model in that self-directedness by the instructional or inquiry models would assume a preference for planning alone (even if the actual learning involved other persons).

A Learning Style?

Table 2:4. Characteristics of SDOL Styles.

Other-Directed Learner	Self-Directed, Instructional Model	Self-Directed, Inquiry Model
Prefers classes and other structured learning experiences.	Prefers classes that allow self-direction.	Prefers learning outside of educational setting or in minimally restrictive educational environment.
Prefers well-structured content.	Prefers well-structured content, but is willing to look for the structure.	Prefers to provide own structure for content even when structure exists.
Accepts amount of detail presented.	Is detailed when planning.	Plans loosely; resists detailed planning.
Can be successful with minimal study skills and a fair degree of persistence.	Requires considerable skill in instructional planning, especially if done in a context in which a teacher must approve the plan.	Requires skill in recognizing resources available in the environment and in synthesizing information.
Exhibits hostility or panic when expected to do own planning or syntheses of content.	Exhibits hostility or panic when not allowed to participate in planning (especially if the teacher's approaches do not seem logical and organized, when lacks sufficient information to form goals and plans, or when expected to produce content structure during the learning project.	Exhibits hostility of panic when expected to produce specific goals and plans too early in the learning process.

33

Table 2:4 con't. Characteristics of SDOL Styles.

Other-Directed Learner	Self-Directed, Instructional Model	Self-Directed, Inquiry Model
Tends to see pieces of information as unrelated.	Thinks in linear ways and tends to put pieces of information together in linear patterns.	Thinks in holistic ways and tends to put pieces of information into nonlinear patterns.
Prefers learning methods/resources (such as programmed instruction) that provide structure for content.	May prefer some learning methods/resources over others but gives more weight to efficiency and effectiveness of methods when actually learning.	May prefer some learning methods/resources over others and is likely to be more sensitive to availability of preferred ones.
Does not provide own structure for picturing learning projects; sees the structure if the teacher explains it.	Plans projects with narrow scope; sees broader learning goals being achieved by a series of discretely defined projects.	Conducts ongoing, broad projects; not always able to say where one learning project ends and another begins.
Appears successful in class when teacher or context provides adequate structure.	Appears successful in class when knows enough about content to do required planning.	May appear unsuccessful in class if planning is the measure of success; appears successful outside of class because of resourcefulness in finding new information and producing original thoughts.
Has limited number of pragmatic and narrow learning goals.	Has a variety of types of learning goals, but tends to focus on the one goal at a time and to prefer pragmatic goals.	Has great range of learning goals, with several pursued at once; some may be only for the pleasure of learning.

Table 2:4 con't. Characteristics of SDOL Styles.

Other-Directed Learner	Self-Directed, Instructional Model	Self-Directed, Inquiry Model
Meets goals on the schedule set by teacher; learning seems to progress at steady pace.	Learning seems to progress at steady pace, is finished on schedule.	It may not seem at first that much learning is being accomplished; framework emerges suddenly, and disjointed learning gels; that may not happen according to the teacher's schedule.
Likes formal education because it provides a structure and person to direct the learning.	Likes formal education because it provides for orderly planning	Dislikes formal education because it is unnatural.
Does not learn much from the everyday environment.	Learns from the everyday environment only if need is great enough to prompt planning and executing the plan	Learns much from the everyday environment, sometimes without distinguishing between what is relevant and irrelevant.
When hits a snag in carrying out plans, stops and waits for further instructions; may not become frustrated because assumes problem is teacher's to solve.	When hits snag, becomes frustrated and must rework plans before proceeding.	Seldom recognizes snags; just moves on to some other resource that is available.
Tends to be field dependent.	Tends to be field independent.	Tends to be field independent.

Table 2:4 con't. Characteristics of SDOL Styles.

Other-Directed Learner	Self-Directed, Instructional Model	Self-Directed, Inquiry Model
As measured by Myers-Briggs Type Indicator, tends to be extravert.	Tends to prefer judging and sensing.	Tends to prefer perceiving and intuition.
May be either left-brained or right brained, as measure by an instrument like the Human Information Processing Survey.	Tends to be left-brained.	Tends to be right-brained.
As measured by Kolb Learning Style Inventory, tends to be converger.	Tends to be a converger.	Tends to be diverger, assimilator, or accomodator.
As measured by the D-Scale, tends to be closed minded	Tends to be open minded, but not as much so as one who follows inquiry model.	Tends to be open minded.

<u>Where does motivation fit into this model</u>? Some persons may not be motivated to learn; they are non-learners. Even other-directed learners, however, should be assumed to provide their own motivation, as should self-directed learners. This assumption is made largely because of intended uses for a style-measurement questionnaire.

<u>How might an SDOL instrument be used</u>? This question is debated in relation to existing learning style instruments, and the same issues seem to be at stake in relation to SDOL. It is this reader's view (Bonham, 1987) that the most defensible use is education of learners about their own styles, so that they can work toward style-flexing (using whatever style is most productive in a given context). Assuming such use, it seems a non-learner (one lacking proper motivation) would be further alienated by having the lack of proper motivation pointed out when an instrument is interpreted. Furthermore, few non-learners would complete the questionnaire or have their styles explained, because of the voluntary nature of most adult education. It seems counter-productive, then, to propose a non-learner or unmotivated style or to plan an instrument that would measure motivation. This line of reasoning speaks against a major thrust of existing instruments, which do emphasize motivation.

An SDOL instrument would be useful in carrying out Smith's (1988) detailed proposal for teaching self-directed learning as a component of learning to learn. A learning-style approach would put into perspective several equally valuable ways of learning, would lead to defining and teaching skills needed for all of those ways, and would encourage the conscious choice of learning approaches for individual situations.

<u>How are opposites accounted for in this model</u>? Given earlier statements about the need for defining opposing styles, one would expect to see opposites defined in this theory. The preceding discussion has ruled out the motivated / unmotivated (learner/non-learner) polarity. Other-directed learning contrasts with self-directed learning (by either model), and the two kinds of self-directed learning contrast with each other.

CONCLUSIONS

This paper has sought to show that self-directed orientation toward learning (SDOL) may be a learning style--a relatively stable preference for certain approaches to learning. At this stage of theory development, this point is more important than the details about possible style elements.

There is evidence that some researchers think of SDOL as if it were a style. Such thought is underscored by the development of instruments to measure how self-directed one person is in relation to another. These instruments, however, may identify learners versus non-learners, instead of self-directed learners versus other-directed learners. Furthermore, they do not distinguish persons who like to learn in an organized self-directed way from those who like to learn in a more free-form fashion.

To develop SDOL as a learning style theory, two concepts must be given greater attention than has been done so far. Opposites must be clearly defined (rather than just defining SDOL as a more-to-less continuum). All style elements identified in that process must be viewed as useful in some contexts (rather than saying more of SDOL is always better than less).

The proposed model of SDOL as a learning style includes three styles: other-directed learning, which contrasts with self-directed learning; and two kinds of self-directed learning, which contrast with each other. Each has positive and negative aspects, and each is likely to be most useful in a different situation. Cognitive and personality characteristics and other learning styles are suggested as correlates of the various SDOL styles. The possibility is also raised that there are six styles instead of three: preference for a level or kind of self-direction may be different if expressed in a non-educational context than in an educational one.

The need to develop a learning-style model in relation to self-directed learning can be seen in surveying the fields of theory and practice. The definition of self-directed learning may be sharpened by determining how individuals prefer to function in a variety of learning settings; it may also be sharpened by better defining the learning approaches in opposition to various kinds of self-directedness and by defining the positive uses of a number of these learning approaches. Where practitioners are ready to teach skills needed for self-directed learning, these improved conceptualizations can be used in practice, for interpreting individuals to themselves and as the basis for planning skills training.

REFERENCES

Bonham, L.A. (1987). Theoretical and practical differences and similarities among selected cognitive and learning styles of adults: An analysis of the literature. Unpublished doctoral dissertation, University of Georgia.

Bowes, S.G., & Smith, R.M. (1986). Directing your own continuing education. Lifelong Learning, 9 (8), 8-10.

Brockett, R. (1983). Self-directed learning and the hard-to-reach adult. Lifelong Learning: The Adult Years, 6 (8), 16-18.

Brockett, R.G. (1985). Methodological and substative issues in the measurement of self-directed learning readiness. Adult Education Quarterly, 36, 15-24.

Brookfield, S. (1984). Self-directed adult learning: A critical paradigm. Adult Education Quarterly, 35, 59-71.

Brookfield, S. (1986). Understanding and facilitating adult learning. San Francisco: Jossey-Bass Publishers.

Brookfield, S. (1988). Conceptual, methodological and practical ambiguities in self-directed learning. In H. B. Long & Associates, Self-directed learning: Application and theory. Athens, GA: Adult Education Department, University of Georgia. 11-37.

Caffarella, R.S., & Caffarella, E.P. (1986). Self-directedness and learning contracts in adult education. Adult Education Quarterly, 36, 226-234.

Caffarella, R.S., & O'Donnell, J.M. (1988). Research in self-directed learning: Past, present and future trends. In H.B. Long & Associates, Self-directed learning: Application and theory. Athens, GA: Adult Education Department, University of Georgia. 39-61.

Carpenter, M.G. (1981). Self-actualizing and other selected characteristics of adults enrolled in correspondence study: A comparative study. Dissertation Abstracts International, 42, 2435A-2436A.

Claxton, C.B., & Ralston, Y. (1978). Learning styles: Their impact on teaching and administration. (AAHE-ERIC/Higher Education Research Report No. 10). Washington, DC: American Association for Higher Education (ERIC Document Reproduction Service No. ED 167 065)

Cobb, J.E. (1979). Self-directed learning of prospective parents. Dissertation Abstracts International, 39, 2684A.

Danis, C., & Tremblay, N.A. (1988). Autodidactic learning experiences: Questioning established adult learning principles. In H.B. Long & Associates, Self-directed learning: Application and theory. Athens, GA: Adult Education Department, University of Georgia. 171-197.

DeRoos, K.K.B. (1982). Persistence of adults in independent study. Dissertation Abstracts International, 43, 47A.

Even, M.J. (1978, April). Overview of cognitive styles and hemispheres of the brain research, and Interpolation of cognitive styles and hemispheres of the brain research into adult education terminology toward formulation of research hypotheses (A two-part paper). Paper presented at the meeting of the Adult Education Research Conference, San Antonio, TX.

Geisler, K.K. (1985). Learning efforts of adults undertaken for matriculation into a community college. Dissertation Abstracts International, 45, 2737A-2738A.

Gibbons, M., Bailey, A., Comeau, P., Schmuck, J., Seymour, S., & Wallace, D. (1980). Toward a theory of self-directed learning: A study of experts without formal training. Journal of Humanistic Psychology, 20 (2), 41-56.

Gross, R., Tough, A., Hebert, T. (1978). Independent, self-directed learners in American life: The other 80% of learning. Yearbook of adult and continuing education, 1978-79 (pp. 43-77). Chicago: Marquis Academic Media.

Guglielmino, L.M. (1978). Development of the Self-Directed Learning Readiness Scale (Doctoral dissertation, University of Georgia, 1977). Dissertation Abstracts International, 38, 6467A.

Hassan, A.M. (1982). An investigation of the learning projects among adults of high and low readiness for self-direction in learning. Dissertation Abstracts International, 42, 3838A-3839A.

Hiemstra, R. (1976). The older adult's learning projects. Educational Gerontology, 1, 331-341.

Hiemstra, R. (1985). The older adult's learning projects. In D.B. Lumsden (Ed.), The older adult as learner: Aspects of educational gerontology. Washington, DC: Hemisphere Publishing Corporation. 165-196.

Hiemstra, R. (1988). Self-directed learning: Individualizing instruction. In H.B. Long & Associates, Self-directed learning: Application and theory. Athens, GA: Adult Education Department, University of Georgia. 99-124.

Houle, C.E. (1961). The inquiring mind. Madison, WI: The University of Wisconsin Press.

Kasworm, C.E. (1983-1984). An examination of self-directed contract learning as an instructional strategy. Innovative Higher Education, 8, 45-54.

Kasworm, C.E. (1988). Self-directed learning in institutional contexts: An exploratory study of adult self-directed learners in higher education. In H.B. Long & Associates, Self-directed learning: Application and theory. Athens, GA: Adult Education Department, University of Georgia. 65-97.

Kathrein, M.A. (1981). A study of self-directed continued professional learning of members of the Illinois Nurses' Association: Content and process. Dissertation Abstracts International, 42, 1902A.

Keefe, J.W. (1979). Learning style: An overview. In J.W. Keefe (Ed.), Student learning styles: Diagnosing and prescribing programs. Reston, VA: National Association of Secondary School Principals. 1-17

Knowles, M.S. (1975). Self-directed learning: A guide for learners and teachers. New York: Association Press.

Kolb, D.A. (1976). Learning style inventory technical manual. Boston: McBer and Combany.

Long, H.B. (1985). Independence in self-directed learning: A conceptual analysis. Paper presented at Region III Conference of National University Continuing Education Association, Knoxville, TN, October 1985.

Long, H.B. (1986a). Self-direction in learning: Conceptual difficulties. Lifelong Learning Forum, 3 (1), 1-2.

Long, H.B. (1986b). Test-retest reliability of Guglielmino's Self-Directed Learning Readiness Scale: A summary report. Working paper, Univ. of Georgia, Adult Education Dept.

Long, H.B., & Agyekum, S.K. (1983). Guglielmino's Self-Directed Learning Readiness Scale: A validation study. Higher Education, 12, 77-87.

Long, H.B., & Agyekum, S.K. (1984). Teacher ratings in the validation of Guglielmino's Self-Directed Learning Readiness Scale. Higher Education, 13, 709-715.

Merriam, S.B. (1986). Adult learning theory: A review of the literature. (Contract No. OERI-P-86-3016). Washington, D.C.: Office of Higher Education & Adult Learning of the Office of Educational Research & Improvement.

Mocker, D.W., & Spear, G.E. (1982). Lifelong learning: Formal, nonformal, informal, and self-directed. Columbus, OH: The ERIC Clearinghouse on Adult, Career, & Vocational Education; The National Center for Research in Vocational Education, The Ohio State University. (Eric Document Reproduction Service No. 220 723)

Oddi, L.F. (1985). Development of an instrument to measure self-directed continuing learning. (Doctoral dissertation, Northern Illinois University, 1984). Dissertation Abstracts International, 46, 49A-50A.

Oddi, L.F. (1986). Development and validation of an instrument to identify self-directed continuing learners. Adult Education Quarterly, 36, 97-107.

Penland, P. (1979). Self-initiated learning. Adult Education, 29, 170-179.

Penland, P. (1981). Towards self-directed learning theory. (ERIC Document Reproduction Service No. 209 475)

Peters, J.M., & Gordon, R.S. (1974). Adult learning projects: A study of adult learning in urban and rural Tennessee. Knoxville, TN: University of Tennessee. (ERIC Document Reproduction Service No. ED 102 431)

Reed, A.W. (1980). Relationship of selected demographic characteristics of adult learners and academic success in a self-directed learning program. Dissertation Abstracts International, 41, 900A-901A.

Rymell, R.G., & Newsom, R. (1981). Self-directed learning and HRD. Training & Development Journal, 35 (8), 50-52.

Sabbaghian, Z. (1980). Adult self-directedness and self-concept: An exploration of relationship. Dissertation Abstracts International, 40, 3701A-3702A.

Savoie, M.L. (1979). Continuing education for nurses: Predictors of success in courses requiring a degree of learner self-direction. Dissertation Abstracts International, 40, 6114A.

Smith, R.M. (1988). Improving dissemination of knowledge about self-directedness in education. In H.B. Long & Associates, Self-directed learning: Application and theory. Athens, GA: Adult Education Department, University of Georgia. 149-167.

Spear, G. (1988). Beyond the organizing circumstances: A search for methodology for the study of self-directed learning. In H.B. Long & Associates, <u>Self-directed learning: Application and theory</u>. Athens, GA: Adult Education Department, University of Georgia. 199-221.

Spear, G.E., & Mocker, D.W. (1984). The organizing circumstance: Environmental determinants in self-directed learning. <u>Adult Education Quarterly</u>, 35, 1-10.

Tough, A. (1971). <u>The adult's learning projects: A fresh approach to theory and practice in adult education</u>. Toronto: The Ontario Institute for Studies in Education.

Tough, A. (1978). Major learning efforts: Recent research and future directions. <u>Adult Education</u>, 28, 250-263.

Wiley, K.R. (1981). Effects of a self-directed learning project and preference for structure on the self-directed learning readiness of baccalaureate nursing students. <u>Dissertation Abstracts International</u>, 43, 49A-50A.

Chapter Three

SELF-DIRECTION AND PROBLEM SOLVING: THEORY AND
METHOD

John M. Peters

One of the few themes in the adult education literature is that much
of adult learning is practically-motivated. This often means that
adults employ learning strategies in order to solve problems in their
lives. While not all learning activities are undertaken by adults who
have an intent to resolve problematic situations, problem-related
learning may be especially prevalent in cases involving largely self-
directed learning activities. In such cases, adults choose to learn in
order to reach goals. When learning is seen as a part of a process
leading to the achievement of a goal, it may also be seen as a
component of a problem solving process. This is why anyone who is
interested in studying self-direction in learning should be concerned
with understanding problem solving processes. This paper overviews
selected descriptions of problem solving, along with closely related
concepts of reasoning and thinking. The paper also discusses
implications for choosing a method for studying self-direction in
learning in the context of problem solving processes.

Self-Direction in Learning
Self-direction in learning is a process in which the learner makes a
decision to learn in order to achieve a goal, formulates a plan to reach
the goal, and takes action toward the goal. Implicit in this definition
is an element of control (Spear, 1988; Chene, 1983; Cheren, 1983).
Self-direction means that the learner has control over the process of
goal setting, planning, and action. This definition excludes situations
in which an external agent such as teacher or book effectively controls
the process described. The person engaged in a learning project may
therefore be in control of the process at some times in the life of the
project, but not at other times, such as when participation in an
organized (by others) learning experience becomes a part of the
project.
    The emphasis in this definition on goal, planning, and action
brings it in line with most descriptions of problem solving processes.
Problem solving can be described in terms of the problem involved
and the process of solving it. A problem, according to Dunder (1945,

p. 5) "...arises when a living organism has a goal but does not know how this goal is to be reached." The process of solving problem involves defining the problem in terms of the discrepancy between the goal and situation, making a plan to solve the problem, and taking action in order to reach the goal. Thus, self-direction in learning may be seen as a problem solving process in its own right, or at least a part of a process of solving problems.

<u>Well-Defined and Ill-Defined Problems</u>
All problems are not alike, however, and the process of solving them may not be the same for all problems. One of the important distinguishing features of problems is the distinction between "well-defined" and "ill-defined" problems. In a well-defined problem, the solution is the same for all problem solvers. The essential conditions of the problem are known. Examples are problems in geometry, the game of Chess, and puzzles such as the well-known "Tower of Hanoi" used in problem solving experiments. On the other hand, an ill-defined problem requires the active participation of the problem solver for its specification; that is, the problem solver largely determines what the problem is and what will count as a solution (Hayes, 1978). Since most "self-directed" learning involves a search for solutions to problems in home, work or social settings, it is safe to assume that such problems are usually ill-defined.

Until recently, research in the area of problem solving focused on well-defined problems in attempts to develop formal models of problem solving processes (Tuma and Reif, 1980; Schon, 1983). Researchers typically engaged subjects in playing games, solving puzzles or computing math problems, and sought to identify patterns of responses that indicated processes of thinking. A classic example of this approach was the work by Newell and Simon (1972) who set out to identify a small set of general problems solving structures that could be applied to a broad range of problems. Their "general problem solving" (GPS) methodology involved presenting a subject with a problem (e.g., the Tower of Hanoi) and asking that the subject "think out loud" as he/she worked through the problem. The resultant transcript of the subject's verbalizations was analyzed for heuristics which were effective in the solution of the problem. The researchers were interested in developing computer models of the problem solving process. When presented with relatively simple problems, the GPS proceeded to straightforwardly apply rules to the problem domain in a trial and error fashion, and thus "worked" in tightly-circumscribed problem domains. With increasing problem complexity, however, the GPS became less successful. In other words, while the GPS seemed to work with well-defined problems whose rules were easily transferable to computer models, it had limited generalizability to ill-defined problem domains.

There has been a shift in more recent years from a concern with well-defined problems to a focus on ill-defined problems, and from a search for global rules of problem solving to an elaboration of the influence of the problem situation. Concomitant with this shift has been greater attention to the role that personal experience and detailed domain knowledge play in problem solving (Peters, Johnson and Lazzara, 1981). Winograd (1980) identified the primary reason for this shift in focus, when he claimed that "We cannot look to simple notions of truth and deduction for problem definition" (p. 237). He was speaking about the proclivity of researchers for formal models of problem solving, although in his view, "social reality is indeterminate" (p. 237), and what is "real" or "true" about it is only relative to a given community. In everyday reality, purpose and context help determine the solutions that are appropriate to solving a problem in the same way that they determine the meaning of words in a sentence. Winogard argued that:

> In looking at any significant sample of natural language, it becomes quickly apparent that only a small amount of human "reasoning" fits the mold of deductive logic. One is often presented with a fragmentary description of some object or situation, and on the basis of knowledge of what is "typical" jumps to a number of conclusions that are not justifiable as logical deductions, and may at times be false. Most (formal systems of problem solving) have been based on a notion of deduction that does not account for this style of reasoning (p. 219).

Thus, if we wish to understand how a person solves a problem we must begin an understanding of the background assumptions that structure the problem context for that person. Reasoning is also to be understood in this way.

Reasoning

Reasoning, explained by Angel (1964, p. 2) is "...the kind of mental activity in which an individual is trying to arrive at a conclusion on the basis of reasons." Reasoning occurs whenever we draw inferences, or go beyond information given. "Reasoning can be seen as fundamental to virtually all cognitive acts from social judgments to language comprehension" (Evans, 1983, p. 6). Angel (1964, p. 3) emphasizes four points about the nature of reasoning:

1. Reasoning is a process, and one with a purpose. It is a process of "trying" to "arrive at a conclusion..." Reasoning will only begin where someone has an unanswered, unsolved question or problem and is looking for something on which to "base" a conclusion even though he doesn't know yet what his conclusion will be.

2. The solution sought by reasoning is of a special kind, to be arrived at in a special manner. One is seeking to arrive, specifically, at "a conclusion on the basis of reasons"...which specifies both the goal and the method followed in reasoning.

3. Reasoning belongs only to individuals. It cannot be transferred, though its description can.

4. Reasoning is considered as a mental, inward activity.

This set of characteristics makes reasoning a species of problem solving, or at least a part of any problem solving process. The focus here is on reasoning as a purposive action, used in situations in which the individual is aware that he/she doesn't have a solution to a problem, but is trying to arrive at one based on reasons. Argyris (1982) lends further support to this view by claiming that "People rarely produce actions that do not make sense to themselves; they have intentions about what it is they are trying to accomplish" (p. 41), and "All actions that have intended consequences are based on reasoning" (p. 470).

Reasoning as problem solving can be carried as formal, or syllogistic reasoning, or it can be carried out informally. Informal reasoning plays a crucial role in solving everyday problems, i.e., those earlier referred to as ill-defined. In both types of reasoning, there is an implied <u>argument</u> <u>structure</u>. That is, when people reason, they effectively develop an argument to support a point of view or a solution alternative, and they may offer up the argument when they explain their reasoning to other people. However, the two types of arguments are to be judged differently in terms of their "validity". Whereas in traditional logical reasoning models all that is relevant is that the syllogisms involved be truth preserving, the informal argument is judged in terms of the felicity of its premises, or the sensibility or appropriateness of reasons associated with the argument.

A "practical argument" is a verbalization of practical reasoning, which is reasoning about what to do (Anscombe, 1978). For example: "I want to travel abroad. In order to travel abroad I need money. I shall get money." When a practical argument is offered to others as support for one's own actions, the person giving it usually describes it in terms of what Von Wright (1963), Dennett (1983) and Coulter (1980) refer to as the "intentional idiom", or the "grammar of intentionality." The intentional idiom is the language used when one gives reasons for things that one has done or plans to do. A person's accounts of actions refer to such things as his/her beliefs about the world, purposes or intentions, wants and desires, and the rules of conduct he/she abides by at any given time.

Thinking
Thinking is closely related to both reasoning and problem solving, especially when viewed in the context of action. Reasoning can be seen as a kind of thinking, although not all kinds of thinking are reasoning. Examples of thinking that are not reasoning include thinking about past experiences (remembering), thinking about the future, or merely describing an event, especially if these thoughts are not intended to be extended or related to other thoughts. The distinction here is based on what Gilhooy (1982) calls directive thinking vs. undirected thinking. The former type of thinking is directed toward some end or goal and the latter involves undirected thought, such as daydreaming. Gilhooy quotes Hobbes on this subject:

> This train of thoughts, or mental discourse, is of two sorts. The first is unguided, without design, and inconstant...In which case the thoughts are said to wander, and seem impertinent (unrelated) one to another....And yet, in this wild ranging of the mind, a man may ofttimes perceive the way of it, and the dependence of one thought upon another...the second is more constant, as being regulated by some desire, and design (Gilhooy, p. 104).

Definitions of thinking generally refer to mental models or mental processes, such as Gilhooly's. Thinking, he says, refers to "...a set of processes whereby people assemble, use and revise internal symbolic models. These models may be intended to represent reality (as in science) or conceivable reality (as in fiction) or even be quite abstract with no particular interpretation intended (as in music or pure mathematics)" (p. 1). Some theorists and philosophers have argued that thinking is both directive and contemplative in nature, and that both have roles to play in problem solving actions. For example, Castaneda (1975) ties the two together in terms of what he calls "practical thinking", or "...finding out or deciding what to do, as well as in helping other to decide or learn what to do" (p. 5). In fact, thinking what to do with oneself or what another is to do, according to Castaneda, are examples of the "practical uses of reasoning" (p. 6).

Philosophers who focus on everyday experience as the subject of their analyses at least implicitly refer to practical thinking and reasoning. Heidegger, Merleau-Ponty and Wittgenstein are among those who believe that understanding is a matter of knowing how to find one's way about in the world, rather than knowing a lot of facts and rules for relating them (Dreyfus and Dreyfus, 1986). They are said to distinguish between two types of knowing: "knowing that" and "knowing how". Knowing that refers to the store of rules, norms, and facts that are generally assumed to be the person's "knowledge base", while knowing how is intuitive in nature. Dreyfus and Dreyfus offer this definition of knowing how:

> Intuition or know-how, as we understand it, is neither wild guessing nor supernatural inspiration, but the sort of ability we all use all the time as we go about our everyday tasks. (p. 29)

Knowing how has been referred to elsewhere as "operative knowledge" (Johnson, Johnson and Little, 1984). Operative knowledge is different from textbook knowledge, and it is thought to be the kind of knowledge organized to do tasks. It is operative knowledge that allows a person to plan, to decide, to take goal-directed action. Imbedded in this notion of operative knowledge are the concepts of practical reasoning, practical thinking, and practical arguments, discussed above. They are related in the sense that all describe processes of goal directed, intentional action by people operating in problematic situations. It is in this same sense that self-directed learning as intentional problem solving is to be understood.

Toward Method

A concern with the structure of a person's intentionality forms the basis of Harre and Secord's (1973) proposal that theory and research in the study of social reality should concern "self-directed and self-monitored behavior...the prototype of behavior in ordinary living" (p. 9). Self-directed behavior is self-reflective behavior. These authors claim that an explanation of behavior lies in the identification of "generative mechanisms." These mechanisms "drive" behavior via a "self-direction according to the meaning ascribed to the situation" (p. 6). If these generative mechanisms are a function of the meaning of a situation for that person, it follows that one very direct way of accessing these meaning is by gathering first-person accounts of that person's behavior. An analysis of such reports ought to put as in a position to discover the underlying structure of meaning for the person.

Following Harre and Secord's argument, the most direct route to understanding self-direction in learning is to produce models or representations of the structure of the underlying basis--the generative source--of learner performance in learning situations. It is becoming increasingly clear that this underlying basis is not to be found in traditional notions of mental abilities, but rather in specific operative knowledge which has been acquired in order to perform learning tasks (Dreyfus and Dreyfus, 1986). The goal of research in this area should be to describe and represent the cognitive events which take place in solving and learning to solve problems under one's own direction.

In order to achieve this goal, it is necessary to devise a method which will allow the establishment of an empirical basis for understanding operative knowledge in conducting learning/problem solving activities. The most promising approach toward this end, has as its basic assumption the idea that learner reasoning is purposive, and that the knowledge which serves as the basis for learner actions is (or at least can be represented by the investigator as if it were) propositional in nature. Within this framework, it is assumed that an understanding of learner reasoning can be derived from evidences of the information that learners attend to, the meaning which learners attach to this information, and the (implicit or explicit) beliefs, rules and wants which relate these meanings to various decisions or actions which can be taken in learning situations (Harre and Secord, 1973). In other words, the process of reasoning may be uncovered by tracing a learner's answers to, and process of finding answers to, such implicit questions as "What is going on here", "What should I do?" and "Why should I do this?" when they are asked in the context of problematic situations.

A concern with the learner's own interpretation of actual problem situations implicates a phenomenological method of doing research in this area. Phenomenalists are interested in describing and understanding the life-world of people, in terms of the themes that constitute their meaning structures. Themes are recurring ideas, actions and ways of thinking that characterize the individual's relationship with their world. Descriptions are taken directly from the individuals whose meanings are to be understood, and these descriptions are reduced to their essential psychological meaning.

An interview is the most commonly used method for obtaining phenomenological descriptions. The data consist of verbal accounts of events, actions, situations, interactions, feelings, and so forth, taken from the point of view of the interviewee. Data are searched for themes that may initially be implicit in the experiences of the interviewee, but which can be made explicit through description and disciplined reflection. Whereas the structure of meaning between the interviewee and their world may be not have been reflected upon prior to the interview, the interview experience itself is designed to bring prereflective experiences to the level of reflective awareness. This allows the interviewer to probe more deeply into the interviewee's structure of meaning, which in turn provides both the interviewee and interviewer with more context for reflection and further probing. This process of describing and reflecting continues throughout the account of the problem solving experience, until the interviewer is satisfied that the interviewee's underlying generative source of assumptions has been described. It is at this point (and only at this point) in the process that the interviewer's own interpretation may be placed on the meanings expressed by the interviewee.

A method developed by this author and Lazzara (1984) has been used to collect accounts of problem solving experiences by adults in a variety of situations. The Action-Reason-Thematic (ART) method, described in detail elsewhere (Peters, 1988), consists of an interview-analysis-interview cycle. The interview seeks a problem solver's description of his/her approach to solving an actual problem, including reasons for taking particular actions. The interview is iterative, with initial interview results informing later interviews. Each interview protocol is analyzed in terms of specific actions and underlying beliefs, rules, wants and factual information expressed by interviewees as they account for their problem solving experience.

Using an argument analysis procedure developed by Nolt (1984), each action and its supporting network of reasons are examined for both expressed and "hidden" premises, and the latter are made explicit in subsequent interviews. When the argument structures are made complete, they are further examined for underlying themes, which take the form of recurring expressions of beliefs, rules and wants. These are taken to represent the meaning structure that informs the person's problem solving actions. This same method can be used to describe and understand the generative sources of actions taken by adults to direct their own learning experiences.

Guided by assumptions discussed in this paper, the method is being used by this author and his graduate students to uncover answers to such questions as the following:

1. What is the documentary or situational information utilized by a learner in making decisions -- the aspects of a situation which the learner attends to or ignores?

2. What are the kinds of additional information which the learner seeks, or which the learner provides out of his own knowledge, given a problem?

3. How does the learner attempt to recast or transform a problem he/she is called upon to solve in order to relate it to their own experience?

4. What are the goals or purposes served by different learner actions and decisions, and the rationales related to these goals?

5. What are the premises or lines of reasoning on which the learner bases his/her decisions?

6. What are the general or high-level strategies which a learner employs in the conduct of making decisions?

7. What are the short-cuts, percepts and rules of thumb which guide many of the learner's actions?

These questions address descriptions of self-direction in learning that are missing in current literature. The mode of understanding described in this paper seems particularly suited to such questions.

REFERENCES

Angell, R. (1964). Reasoning and logic. New York: Meridith.

Anscombe, G. (1978). Intention. Oxford: Blackwell.

Argyris, C. (1982). Reasoning, learning, and action. San Francisco: Jossey-Bass.

Castaneda, H. (1975). <u>Thinking and doing: The philosophical foundations of institutions</u>. Dordrecht, Holland: D. Reidel.

Chene, A. (1983). The Concept of autonomy: A philosophical discussion. <u>Adult Education Quarterly</u>, 34, 38-47.

Cheren, M. (1983). Helping learners achieve greater self-direction. In R.M. Smith (Ed), <u>Helping Adults Learn How To Learn</u>. San Francisco: Jossey-Bass, Inc.

Coulter, J. (1980). <u>The social construction of mind</u>. Totowa, N.J.: Rowan and Littlefield.

Dennett, D. (1983). Intentional systems in cognitive ethology: The panglossian paradigm defended. <u>The Behavioral and Brain Sciences</u>. New York: Cambridge University Press.

Dreyfus, H. and Dreyfus, S. (1986). <u>Mind over machine</u>. New York: Free Press.

Dunder, K. (1945). On problem solving. <u>Psychological Monographs</u>, 58, No. 270, 1-113.

Evans, J. (1983). <u>Thinking and reasoning: Psychological approaches</u>. London: Routledge & Kegan Paul.

Gilhooly, K. (1982). <u>Thinking: Directed, undirected and creative</u>. London: Academic Press.

Harre R. & Secord, P. (1973). <u>The explanation of social behavior</u>. Totota, N.J.: Littlefield, Adams.

Hayes, J. (1978). <u>Cognitive psychology</u>. Homewood, Ill.: Dorsey Press.

Johnson-Laird, P. (1983). Thinking as a skill. In J. St. B.T. Evans, <u>Thinking and reasoning: Psychological approaches</u>. London: Routledge & Kegan Paul.

Lazzara, P. J. (1985). <u>Foundations for a method for knowledge analysis</u>. Unpublished Ph.D. dissertation, University of Tennessee.

Long, H. and Associates. (1988). <u>Self-directed learning: Application & theory</u>. Athens, Ga., University of Georgia.

Nolt, J. E. (1984). <u>Informal logic: Possible worlds and imagination</u>. New York: McGraw-Hill Company.

Peters, J. (1988). Toward a new procedure for learning project research. Paper presented at AERC/SCUTREA Research Conference, Leeds, UK, July.

Peters, J., Johnson, M., & Lazzara, P. (1981). Adult problem solving and learning Paper presented at American Educational Research Association Conference, Los Angeles.

Schon, D.A. (1983). <u>The reflective practitioner: How professionals think in action</u>. New York: Basic Books.

Spear, G. (1988). Beyond the organizing circumstances: A search for methodology for the study of self-directed learning. In H. Long and Associates <u>Self-directed learning: Application & theory</u>. Athens, Ga., The University of Georgia.

Tuma, D.T. and Reif, F. (1980). <u>Problem solving and education: Issues in teaching and research</u>. Hillsdale, N.J.: Lawrence Erlbaum Associates.

von Wright, G. (1963). <u>Norm and action</u>. New York: Humanities Press.

Winograd, T. (1980). What does It mean To understand language? <u>Cognitive Science</u>, 4, 209-241.

Chapter Four

FACILITATING SELF-DIRECTED LEARNING:
NOT A CONTRADICTION IN TERMS

D. Randy Garrison

Self-directed learning is one of the few areas of research in adult education with an extensive research-based body of knowledge. While we have gained considerable understanding of his long existing phenomenon, the preoccupation with defining and describing self-directed learning may have prevented an adequate exploration of the means of facilitating it. Caffarella and O'Donnell (1987) have stated that of the various categories of research on self-directed learning, little emphasis has been given to questions concerning the role of the adult educator.

Considering this lack of emphasis in facilitating self-directed learning, the purpose of this paper is to explore the importance of this issue and the methods for carrying it out. The first part of the paper will discuss independence in self-directed learning and argue that there is no contradiction in the idea of facilitating self-directed learning. In the second part, the means of facilitating self-directed learning beyond the formal institutional setting will be addressed.

BACKGROUND

Brookfield (1988) has clearly stated his suspicions and doubts concerning the accuracy and utility of this concept and believes "that the over-identification of researchers and practitioners in adult education with the concept of self-directed learning is very dangerous for our field" (p.12). This is largely based on the doubt that self-directed learning is uniquely identified with the adult population. He suggests that we need to recognize the ambiguities in the concept of self-directed learning and goes on to say that the fundamental problem "is the fact that a prescriptive aim (that we should encourage learners' independence) has become confused with an empirically-based proposition (that adult learning styles are inherently self-directed)" (Brookfield, 1988, p.12). To add to the confusion surrounding self-directed learning, Brookfield (1988) also questions the validity of the prescriptive aim of making learners more independent. The position of this paper is that a large portion of the ambiguity surrounding the prescriptive aim of self-directed learning can be attributed to what it means to be independent in an educational transaction.

Intimately related to the idea of independence is the facilitation of self-directed learning in the institutional and noninstitutional setting. According to Long (1988) "there is precious little empirical support for what goes on under the guise of self-directed learning facilitation. The state of affairs is critical when the rapidity at which information is expanding is considered" (p.7). Greater efforts appear to be demanded regarding the facilitation of self-directed learning; but is this counter to the supposed aim of encouraging independence in self-directed learning?

Notwithstanding Brookfield's concerns, it would appear that research in self-directed learning has progressed to the stage where we have sufficient understanding of the nature of the method (i.e., how learning proceeds) to realize that self-directed learners often require help, and yet fail to obtain it. Tough (1979) states that "Many persons would welcome more and better help with their self-planned learning" (p.105) and difficulties in seeking help lead to frustration, confusion, and a lack of motivation. Tough (1979) goes on to suggest that two ways to reduce the difficulties of self-directed learning are to "increase the learner's competence" and "provide much better help". Both of which strongly suggest a role for the adult educator.

Spear and Mocker (1984) have postulated "that self-directed learners, rather than pre-planning their learning projects, tend to select a course from limited alternatives which occur fortuitously within their environment, and which structures their learning projects" (p.4). This might well explain the source of frustration in seeking help suggested by Tough (1979). As Tough (1979) also states, the "freedom to learn whatever one wishes is rather a hollow freedom if there is no opportunity or resource available for learning the chosen subject matter" (p.155). In a discussion of the "organizing circumstances" of self-directed learning Spear (1988) stated it is apparent "that learners seldom considered a variety of alternatives in the selection of resources to use in their projects" (p.201). The issue is whether adult educators accept a deterministic approach to organizing self-directed learning or whether adult educators can or should proactively engage in the facilitation of self-directed learning.

Spear (1988) reports further on a qualitative study of self directed learners originally conducted by Spear and Mocker (1984). With regard to self-directed learning the findings suggested that the "essential elements for understanding the process appeared to be 1) the expectation of the learner, 2) the individual's inventory of skills and knowledge and 3) the particular resources present within the environment" (Spear, 1988, p.202). Clearly, self-directed learning is a complex process that encompasses a number of factors if the self-directed learner is to have control of the learning process and is to achieve the intended outcome in a reasonably effective and efficient manner. However, before exploring the process of self-directed learning further, we must clarify our terminology.

In a critical analysis of self-directed learning Brookfield (1984) states that "one priority for thinkers in this field must be to propose clear and unambiguous definitions of learning and education" (p.61). As a result, some attempt must be made to reduce the confusion resulting from the inadvertent and careless interchange of the terms learning and education. It is assumed here that learning is a broad psychological construct implying internal cognitive and behavioral changes. Education, on the other hand, is restricted to a purposeful, planned, and worthwhile learning activity willingly pursued by the learner. Any reference to learning is viewed within an educational context. As such, all intended and planned forms of learning are considered here as falling within the framework of education.

SELF-DIRECTION AND CONTROL

Closely related to the confusion surrounding learning and education is what we mean by self-direction. Self-direction in learning can be very misleading if we mean that the learner is entirely independent. The view that self-directed learning is a fully self-instructional process has been seriously questioned. Many educators have raised doubts that learning in general, and especially educational activities, take place in isolation (Brookfield, 1985; Chene, 1983; Collins, 1987; Moore, 1973). While at first glance it may seem somewhat contradictory, nonetheless, self-directed learning involves external guidance and support.

The position of this paper is that education is inherently a collaborative and active process between teacher and student. In this transaction the ideas and perspectives of both teacher and student are critically examined and transformed through sustained two-way communication. According to Brookfield (1986) education is a transactional dialogue "where the comments and contributions of the participants build organically on each others views and in which alternative viewpoints, differing interpretations, and criticisms are elements essential to the encounter" (p.23). Given this description of the educational process there is the question of what we mean by independence and in what sense is it desirable. Perhaps the best statement in this regard is provided by Chene (1983) when she states that we tend to "forget that knowledge and skill competency are social products. The value of independence or self-reliance is an illusion and adults are trapped in other forms of dependence if they are not aware of the necessity of mediation by others and of recognition in learning" (p.46).

It has often been said that self-directed learners have assumed responsibility for their own learning. But what exactly does this mean? Candy (1987) states that "I am firmly convinced that adults are responsible for their own learning, but what I have come to reconsider is whether all should be responsible for their own teaching" (p.173). To assume responsibility is to be responsible. To be responsible in an educational sense is to be aware not only of ones own needs and abilities but what are worthwhile goals, appropriate standards, and alternative viewpoints. As interdependent members of a community and society, such issues surrounding self-directed learners are of crucial importance in an educational transaction. Teaching in this sense is an important and necessary component of the educational process.

The issue is to what degree does the self-directed learner take control of the planning and management of the learning process. As Collins (1987) suggests, learning does not take place in a vacuum; mediation is inevitable and "there is no contradiction in the notion that learners do their learning on their own and their being taught by a teacher" (p.80). This is, of course, a crucial issue if we are to discuss the facilitation of self-directed learning. That is to say, we have assumed that facilitating self-directed learning is not a contradiction in terms and it is imperative that we emphasize the understanding of how this can be done.

Unfortunately, self-directed learning "describes a world of opposites: self-directed or other-directed, adult or child, all or nothing... [which] can interfere with a functional approach to the negotiation of roles and can prevent an accurate diagnosis of abilities and needs" (Cheren, 1983, p.25). For this reason Cheren (1983) uses the concept of control and argues, to "achieve greater self-direction in learning is to achieve greater control over one or more aspects of a learning situation" (p.24). The concept of control in the educational transaction, however, needs to be examined more closely.

Garrison and Baynton (1987) have proposed a model (see Figure 4.1) of the educational transaction which goes beyond the concept of independence and self-direction. Central to the model is the concept of control. It is suggested by Garrison and Baynton (1987) that control "is concerned with the opportunity and ability to influence, direct, and determine decisions related to the educational process' (p.5). The three essential dimensions of control are independence, proficiency, and support. Developing and maintaining true control over the educational process is dependent upon establishing a dynamic balance among these dimensions.

Educational independence is the freedom to choose and pursue educational goals without external influence. Such freedom, however, is empty without the proficiency (intellectual, attitudinal, and dispositional abilities) required to achieve the intended educational goals. In addition to freedom and ability to learn is a range of human and nonhuman support resources necessary to reach the educational goal. Within the larger context of teacher, learner and content the dynamic balance of these dimensions of control are manifested in and determined by the communication transaction. In short, control is realized through collaboration between facilitator/teacher and learner/student.

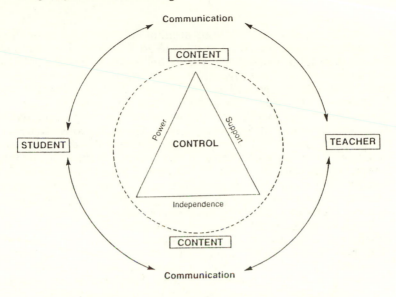

Figure 4.1. Control and the Educational Transaction
(Adapted from Garrison & Baynton, 1987)

It is worth noting the similarity between the three essential elements of the self-directed learning process as previously described by Spear (1988) and the elements of control as defined here. Spear's first element, the expectation of the learner, would appear to address the issue of selecting goals as articulated in "independence". Spear's second element, skills and knowledge, are clearly associated with "proficiency"; while his third element, resources, is obviously associated with the "support" dimension of control. Although the control elements were developed from a distance education framework independent of Spear's typology, the apparent similarity provides empirical support and argues for the validity of the control concept in understanding the self-directed learning process.

In self-directed learning the teacher/facilitator might provide information and guidance where the learner and teacher share control over the educational process. There are many educational situations where the learner would gladly give up some independence for increased support in order to more efficiently and effectively achieve the desired outcome. Paradoxically, by giving up independence for guidance and support the learner gains control in regards to the outcome of the educational experience since the desirable and worthwhile goal will be more apparent and achievable. During the process of learning, control may be seen as being shared. As Tough (1979) states, the "distinction between help and control is important, because it helps us realize that a learner can receive a great deal of help without giving up any of his control or responsibility" (p.192).

The control model is an attempt to reflect the fundamental elements and their interrelationships in an educational transaction. It is important to emphasize that the model is not applicable only to the formal institutional setting. The facilitator (teacher) need not be associated with an institution and be certified to fulfill the essential functions of this role. In addition, content does not have to be possessed by the facilitator. In the most prevalent and naturally occurring form of self-directed learning, all the various elements are likely to be present. The important issues are the dynamic balance among the elements of control as well as the nature and extent of interaction at the macro level between (among) facilitator(s) and learner. For example, independence may be very high if proficiency and support elements are sufficiently present; if not, the learner is likely to seek out a facilitator or resource person to a greater extent.

The educational transaction depicted in Figure 4.1 is made possible through the communication process. Salomon (1981) states that one "could hardly argue with the assertion that education depends on acts of communication" (p.35). Houle (1972) believes that education "is a cooperative rather than an operative art" (p.44); and Brookfield (1986) suggests that the ideal educational process is a "transactional encounter in which learners and teachers are engaged in a continual process of negotiation of priorities, methods, and evaluative criteria" (p.20). It is argued here that control of the educational process is realized through communication between facilitator and learner, and independence is only one element in the transaction.

There are two relatively distinct communication phases in the educational transaction. The first is the planning stage where the triadic relationship between teacher, student, and content predominates. Too often discussion at this stage regarding aims and strategies are very limited or nonexistent. During the second phase instructional issues predominate. The shift is toward the control dimensions and some form of sustained dialogue between teacher and student is crucial. The control possessed by the student is very much dependent upon this communication transaction. The integration and balance between and within each of these phases is dependent upon the communication process.

Before leaving the discussion of control and the educational transaction it is important to address self-direction from both an external and internal perspective. The educational transaction is not just who controls decisions regarding tasks and activities but, perhaps more importantly, it is also concerned with the process of critical reflection and "internal change of consciousness" or "perspective transformation". Self-direction only has meaning, according to Brookfield (1988), when we talk about the external or "educational" activities and has "nothing to do with the internal change of consciousness which result from participation in these acts" (p.19). In the model presented here, the external instructional issues are largely addressed by the dimensions of the control triad. The model does not directly address or order the internal cognitive changes other than to say that they occur through transactional dialogue at both the macro and micro levels.

The dilemma, however, is mapping the relationship and influence of the external educational activities and the internal change of consciousness (i.e., perspective transformation). To begin with, in any educational transaction we cannot control and predict in a one-to-one correspondence (nor would we want to) all legitimate cognitive transformations. Brookfield (1988) speaks of educational encounters as psycho-social dramas where there is spontaneity, serendipity and happenstance but "all within the structure provided by the script" (p.20). Secondly, the issue which goes to the heart of the matter concerns the relationship of external and internal self-directedness. While it may be imagined that an individual can be self-directed by having control over much of the educational environment, it is more difficult to imagine a true educational experience without negotiation of goals, dialogue regarding perspectives, and the validation of knowledge through interaction with a teacher as well as others. To reiterate, education is a purposeful, worthwhile, and collaborative learning experience. It is not learning that can occur autonomously or without the total disregard of societal values and knowledge as reflected by the teacher. The educational transaction will critically examine the ideas and prospectives of both teacher and student.

SELF-DIRECTED AND DISTANCE LEARNING

It has been stated that learning does not take place in isolation, and therefore, control in self-directed learning is dependent upon collaboration and communication. With regard to projects that learners initiate for themselves, Cheren (1983) suggests there are two questions that need to be answered; "(1) How much control will the learner exercise... and (2) to what extent will others be involved" (p.26). To answer these questions requires a holistic view of the educational transaction as depicted in Figure 1. And adult educators need to ask, how do we facilitate the ubiquitous learning activities that we have categorized and labeled as self-directed learning?

It has been argued in the past that self-directed learning afforded no opportunity on the part of the adult educator to influence the learning process (Verner, 1964). However, this is no longer the case as evidenced by the extensive innovations in the field of distance education. Distance education is no longer synonymous with independent correspondence study. Virtually any instructional method is available to the adult educator to reach out to self-directed learners beyond the institutional setting.

Distance education is not and should not be seen as some exotic or distinct form of learning. It is first and foremost education where the teacher and student happen to be in a noncontiguous relationship. From the perspective of adult education, distance education can be described as "a broad set of instructional methods based largely on technologically mediated communication capable of extending the influence of the educator beyond the formal institutional setting for the purposes of benefiting the distance learner through appropriate guidance and support" (Garrison, 1987, p.315).

Distance education is a set of methods available to adult educators that can be used in conjunction with traditional face-to-face methods. There are three major distance education technologies (correspondence, teleconferencing, and computer-based) plus a range of ancillary media that can be used to complete the communication loop (Garrison, 1985). In combination, the technologies and media can be designed to meet a range of communication needs. The technologies can be used to support group or individualized learning; regular or irregular communication based upon student need and control; immediate or delayed feedback; and two-way audio or visual information transmission. Not only is greater access to information possible but sustained support of the learning process is readily available through distance education technologies. Facilitation of self-directed learning is a realistic possibility with the adoption of distance education methods.

CONCLUSION

In a complex and changing society the "perception that one has some measure of personal control over the important areas of his or her physical and social situation has emerged as a fundamental prerequisite of psychological well-being and social adjustment" (Brenders, 1987, p.86). With the importance of continuing learning in an information society it would appear that having some measure of personal control over the learning process is also crucial to the social adjustment and psychological well-being of the individual. Such control does not always exist in the self-directed learning activities undertaken by adults. As we have discussed previously, adult self-directed learners would welcome increased support and therefore control in their learning activities.

Cheren (1983) states that "facilitating the transition to greater self-direction in learning is not well served by throwing out all external structure" (p.35). On the contrary, he argues that self-directed learning "usually takes more careful planning and structure to support the enhancement and expansion of the learner's control over his or her learning or development efforts than is required in more traditional learning contexts" (Cheren, 1983, p.35). Adult educators should become more innovative in meeting the educational needs of self-directed learners through a creative mix of traditional and distance education methods which would facilitate effective student control over their learning. However, before we can begin to create these support systems we must believe that facilitating self-directed learning is important and does not represent a contradiction in terms.

REFERENCES

Brenders, D.A. (1987). Perceived control: Foundations and directions for communication research. In M.L. McLaughlin (Ed.), Communication Yearbook 103. London: Sage Publications. 86-116.

Brookfield, S. (1984). Self-directed adult learning: A critical paradigm. Adult Education Quarterly, 35, 59-71.

Brookfield, S. (1985). Self-directed learning: A critical review of research. In S. Brookfield (Ed.), Self-directed learning: From theory to practice. San Francisco: Jossey-Bass Inc., Publishers. 5-16.

Brookfield, S. (1986). Understanding and facilitating adult learning. San Francisco: Jossey-Bass Publishers.

Brookfield, S.M. (1988). Conceptual, methodological and practical ambiguities in self-directed learning. In H.B. Long and Associates, Self-directed learning: Application & Theory. Athens, Georgia: Adult Education Department, University of Georgia. 1-10.

Caffarella, R.S., & O'Donnell, J.M. (1987). Self-directed adult learning: A critical paradigm revisited. Adult Education Quarterly, 37, 199-211.

Candy, P. (1987). Evolution, revolution or devolution: Increasing learner-control in the instructional setting. In D. Bond & V. Griffin (Eds.), Appreciating adults learning: From the learner's perspective. London: Kogan Page. 159-178.

Chene, A. (1983). The concept of autonomy: A philosophical discussion. Adult Education Quarterly, 34, 38-47.

Cheren, M. (1983). Helping learners achieve greater self-direction. In R.M. Smith (Ed.), Helping adults learn how to learn. San Francisco: Jossey-Bass Inc., Publishers. 23-37.

Collins, M. (1987). Self-directed learning and the misappropriation of adult education practice. In M.A. Gillen & A. Burkholder (Eds.), Canadian Association for the Study of Adult Education Conference Proceedings. 68-85. Antigonish, Nova Scotia: St. Francis Xavier University.

Garrison, D.R. (1985). Three generations of technological innovation in distance education. Distance Education, 6, 235-241.

Garrison, D.R. (1987). Self-directed and distance learning: Facilitating self-directed learning beyond the institutional setting. International Journal of Lifelong Education, 6, 309-318.

Garrison, D.R., & Baynton, M. (1987). Beyond independence in distance education: The concept of control. The American Journal of Distance Education, 3(1), 3-15.

Houle, C.O. (1972). The design of education. San Francisco: Jossey-Bass.

Long, H.B. (1988). Self-directed learning reconsidered. In H.B. Long and Associates, Self-directed learning: Application & Theory. Athens, Georgia: Adult Education Department, University of Georgia. 1-10.

Moore, M. (1973). Toward a theory of independent learning and teaching. Journal of Higher Education, 44, 661-679.

Salomon, G. (1981). Communication and education: Social and psychological interactions. London: Sage Publications.

Spear, G. (1988). Beyond the organizing circumstance: A search for methodology for the study of self-directed learning. In H.B. Long and Associates, Self-directed learning: Application & Theory. Athens, Georgia: Adult Education Department, University of Georgia. 199-221.

Spear, G.E., & Mocker, D.W. (1984). The organizing circumstance: Environmental determinants in self-directed learning. Adult Education Quarterly, 35, 1-10.

Tough, A. (1979). The adult's learning projects: A fresh approach to theory and practice in adult learning (2nd ed.). Toronto: The Ontario Institute for Studies in Education.

Verner, C. (1964). Definition of terms. In G. Jensen, A.A. Liverright, & W. Hallenback (Eds), Adult education: Outlines of an emerging field of university study. Washington, D.C.: Adult Education Association of the U.S.A.. 27-39.

Chapter Five

DEVELOPMENT OF AN ADULT BASIC EDUCATION FORM OF THE SELF-DIRECTED LEARNING READINESS SCALE

Lucy Madsen Guglielmino

Increasing attention has been given to the assessment and development of self-directed learning readiness, especially in the last ten years. The idea that learning how to learn is now the most important skill that one must acquire has been suggested by many, but stated most directly by John Naisbitt (1985). Naisbitt reports that he is often asked, "What subject should I (or my child) study in order to be really prepared for the future?" Naisbitt indicates that people tend to expect a high-tech answer, but his response is:

> In a world that is constantly changing, there is no one subject or set of subjects that will serve you for the foreseeable future, let alone for the rest of your life. The most important skill to acquire now is learning how to learn (Naisbitt's italics). If you know how to learn you can adapt and change no matter what technological, social or economic permutations occur. (p. 133)

NEED FOR A FORM OF THE SELF-DIRECTED LEARNING READINESS SCALE APPROPRIATE FOR USE WITH ADULTS OF LOW EDUCATIONAL ATTAINMENT

The interest in assessing and developing readiness for self-directed learning has led to extensive use of the Self-Directed Learning Readiness Scale, developed and field- tested in 1977 (Guglielmino). The original adult version has been translated into six languages and used in over 150 research efforts. An elementary form with a lower reading level has been available since 1978. However, several studies have suggested a need for a new form designed for adults, but at a lower reading level than the original form.

Brockett (1983, 1985) documented some problems in using the adult form of the SDLRS with older adults of low educational attainment. He administered the adult form by reading it to the adults to overcome the apparent problems with reading level, but still noted that they had problems with the wording of the response options and the reverse items. He reports that Sisco encountered similar difficulties in a study involving rural adults of low educational attainment. Although the difficulties were not mentioned in the report of the study (Leean and Sisco, 1981), they were stated in a personal communication from Sisco to Brockett (1982). Brockett indicated that a third issue relating to the use of the SDLRS with the group was the "items that address issues related to schooling and/or learning acquired through books and study skills." As he indicated, five items of the 58-item SDLRS address this type of learning. For the group of older adults with low educational attainment in his study, three of these five items did not show significant item-test correlations. Brockett saw this as "a strong emphasis on books and schooling" which he felt was inappropriate for adults of low educational attainment. Long (in press) has also reported similar findings that indicate relatively lower item correlations in a sample of older subjects. These concerns led the author to consider designing a new form of the SDLRS for adults of low educational attainment.

DEVELOPMENT OF THE SDLRS-ABE

Since the original form of the SDLRS was based on a carefully-designed survey of abilities, attitudes, and personality characteristics related to self-directed learning, it was decided to use the same content as the basis for the ABE version. Briefly, the format used was a modification of the Delphi technique. Fourteen authorities on self-directed learning participated in a three-round survey, in which they were asked to name and rate attitudes, abilities, values, and personality characteristics which they considered important for self-directed learning. The initial questionnaire included an open-ended listing followed by a checklist of characteristics suggested by the literature. In round two, panel members received a list of responses suggested by all members in round one and rated them on a scale of 1 to 7, with the following points indicated:

> 1 - unnecessary
> 3 - desirable
> 5 - necessary
> 7 - essential.

In round three they were provided with the results of the ratings and were asked to rate the listed attitudes, abilities, and characteristics once more, explaining any response for which their rating fell outside of the semi-interquartile range of the group's ratings for that response.

Thirty-three of the fifty-six characteristics rated in round three emerged with a rating of <u>desirable</u> or higher (median of 3.0 or higher). These characteristics were used as the basis

Table 5.1: Characteristics Rated <u>Desirable</u> or Higher in
the Delphi Survey Arranged in Order from Highest to Lowest
Medians on Round Three

Median	Characteristic
5.2	Initiative
5.1	(Independence (Persistence
4.7	Sense of responsibility for one's own learning
4.6	Tendency to view problems as challenges
4.5	(Self-discipline (High degree of curiosity (Strong desire to learn or change
4.2	(Ability to use basic study skills (Ability to organize one's time and set an appropriate pace for learning (Self-confidence
4.1	(Ability to develop a plan for completing work (Joy in learning
4.0	Tendency to be goal oriented
3.9	(Tolerance of ambiguity (Preference for active participation in shaping educational program (Ability to evaluate own progress (Intellectual responsibility
3.6	Patience
3.4	Ability to diagnose own learning needs
3.2	(Exploratory view of education (Above average risk-taking behavior (Knowledge of a variety of potential learning resources and ability to use them (Ability to accept and use criticism (Ability to discover new approaches for dealing with problems

Median	Characteristic
3.1	(Ability to formulate learning objectives
	(Tendency to be task oriented
	(Ability to select and use many learning strategies
	(Positive orientation to the future
	(Emotional security
3.0	(Average or above average intelligence
	(Creativity
	(Preference for independent study or relatively
	unstructured courses

for item development for the SDLRS. The characteristics and their medians are arranged in order from highest to lowest medians in Table 5.1.

ADDRESSING CONCERNS RAISED IN THE LITERATURE RELATED TO ADULTS OF LOW EDUCATIONAL ATTAINMENT

Since the SDLRS-A, which was developed to measure these characteristics, has been found to be valid and reliable for many populations, (Brookfield, 1984; Brockett, 1985; Long and Agyekum, 1983; Long and Agyekum, 1984; Finestone, 1984), it was decided that the SDLRS-A items would be the starting point for the ABE version. However, the issues raised by Brockett would need to be addressed. The elementary form which was developed in 1978 addressed two of the concerns reported by Brockett: it had a lower reading level and it had simplified response options. (See Table 2).

However, the wording of some of the questions was not appropriate for adults. For example, item #10 reads, "I can learn things by myself better than most kids my age." A simple rewording of the elementary form, then, would address those concerns.

Table 5.2: Response Options for the Adult and Elementary Forms of the Self-Directed Learning Readiness Scale

SDLRS-A	SDLRS-E
1. Almost never true of me; I hardly ever feel this way.	1. I never feel like this.
2. Not often true of me; I feel this way less than half the time.	2. I feel like this only once in a while.
3. Sometimes true of me; I feel this way about half the time.	3. Half the time I feel this way.
4. Usually true of me; I feel this way more than half the time.	4. Usually I feel like this.
5. Almost always true of me; there are very few times when I don't feel this way.	5. I feel like this all the time.

Another concern reported by Brockett and Long (1986) was the difficulty of the reverse items for individuals with low educational attainment. After careful consideration, the author decided to continue the practice of using reverse items in the revised form for adults with low reading levels (SDLRS-ABE). While reverse items do appear to be more difficult for those with low reading levels to understand, there is also a major disadvantage to including no reverse items in a self-report instrument. In self-report instruments in which all items are positively stated, subjects can easily develop a response set (Thorndike and Hagen, 1969; Cronbach, 1971). If every item for two pages is a 4 or a 5 on the response scale, an individual may begin to assume that the remaining responses will be similar and cease to read the items carefully. Including reverse items, while it complicates scoring and may increase reading difficulty, is important in avoiding the development of a response set on a self-report instrument.

The remaining issue is the inclusion of items relating to books and schooling. Brockett's point that much learning takes place in the absence of books and schooling is well-taken; this concept was, in fact a strong consideration in the development of the initial scale.

The instructions to the individuals who participated in the Delphi survey which was used as a basis for determining the content of the items in the SDLRS included this introductory statement on each of the three questionnaires in the survey:

It is the author's assumption that self-directed in learning exists along a continuum; it is present in each person to some degree. In addition, it is assumed that self-direction in learning can occur in a wide variety of situations, ranging from a teacher-directed classroom to self-planned and self-conducted learning projects. Although certain learning situations are more conductive to self-direction in learning than are others, it is the personal characteristics of the learner--including his attitudes, his values, and his abilities--which ultimately determine whether self-directed learning will take place in a given learning situation. The self-directed learner more often chooses or influences the learning objectives, activities, resources, priorities, and levels of energy expenditure than does the other-directed learner. (Guglielmino, 1977, p. 93)

The introduction clearly indicates a view of self-directed learning which is not strongly focused on classrooms and books. Only 5 out of the 58 items of the original scale (8.6%) referred to classrooms, tests, study skills, or libraries. The remaining 53 items (91.4%) referred to altitudes and actions supportive of self-directed learning not tied to any particular setting. The author feels that an instrument in which 91.4% of the items do not relate to books and schooling does not reflect "a strong emphasis on books and schooling" (Brockett, 1985, p. 21).

Since it is a rare individual indeed in our society who has not had some contact with classrooms, and since the five items do not all necessarily refer to the subject as a student in a classroom, it was decided to include the items relating to books and schooling in the field-test version of the SDLRS-ABE and eliminate them only if the item-test correlations were poor.

ADDRESSING CONCERNS RELATED TO NON-NATIVE SPEAKERS OF ENGLISH

Once the concerns reported by Brockett were considered, another important factor was addressed. Our country has absorbed record numbers of immigrants in recent years, and many adults who are enrolled in publicly funded adult basic education (ABE) classes are studying English as a second or third language. Although the percentages would naturally vary from state to state, in Florida, for example, over 50% of the adult basic education students are in classes of English for speakers of other languages (ESOL) (Guglielmino, 1985). During a period of heavy refugee influx in 1979, the percentage was even higher: nearly 70% of the adult basic education students were enrolled in ESOL classes. These facts led the author to consider that, to be maximally useful, the ABE version of the SDLRS should not only reflect a lower reading level for native English speakers; it should also be carefully reworded to avoid idioms and grammar structures which would raise no problems for the native English speaker but would greatly increase the reading difficulty for the non-native speaker.

A final consideration for both native and non-native speakers which has been voiced by a number of researchers in personal communications is the length of the scale. A shorter version would be desirable for adults of low educational attainment if acceptable levels of validity and reliability could be retained.

SDLRS-ABE DEVELOPMENT PLAN

The procedure for the development and field-testing of the SDLRS-ABE is outlined below. Following the outline, the implementation of steps 1-5 is discussed, as well as the proposed tryout procedure.

1. Item construction, based on stated considerations.

2. Item review

3. Item revision, where necessary

4. Assembly of scale

5. Pre-tryout

6. Tryout

7. Item analysis

8. Second review and revision of items

9. Estimation of scale characteristics from item data

   a. mean

   b. standard deviation

   c. reliability

Item Construction
Based on the considerations described previously, the item construction for the SDLRS-ABE involved the following steps:

1. The items generated from the Delphi survey in 1977 and found to be valid and reliable in the original adult form of the SDLRS were used as a basis for the SDLRS-ABE items.

2.   The items were reworded to lower the reading level as much as possible as was done in the SDLRS-E.

3.   The instructions, response wordings, and individual items were checked and reworded as necessary to avoid idioms and grammar structures which might prove difficult for non-native speakers of English.

4.   The reverse items were retained in order to avoid development of a response set.

5.   The five items relating to books and schooling were retained with the understanding that their performance in the field-test would be examined carefully.

Examples of changes made to lower the reading level are listed in Table 5.3. Changes exemplifying the effort to remove idioms and difficult grammatical structures are listed in Table 5.4.

Table 5.3: Examples of Changes Made in SDLRS Items to Lower Reading Level.

SDLRS-A	SDLRS-ABE
Item 7. I believe that thinking about who you are, where you are, and where you are going should be a major part of every person's education.	Item 8. I believe that a big part of my education should be thinking about what kind of person I am and which kinds of things I want to do with my life.
Item 27. I am capable of learning for myself almost any thing I might need to know.	Item 26. I can learn anything I need to know by myself.
Item 39. I think of problems as challenges, not stop signs.	Item 38. A hard problem doesn't stop me.
Item 41. I'm happy with the way I investigate problems.	Item 40. I am really good a solving problems.

Table 5.4: Examples of Changes Made in SDLRS Items to Avoid Idioms and Simplify Language Structures for the Non-native Speaker.*

SDLRS-E	SDLRS-ABE
Response option 2	
I feel like this <u>only once in a while</u>.	I feel like this <u>less than half the time</u>.
Item 8	
I don't work very well <u>on my own</u>.	I don't work very well <u>by myself</u>.
Item 11	
Even if I have a great idea, I can't <u>figure out how to</u> make it work.	Even if I have a great idea, I can't <u>find a way to</u> make it work.
Item 45	
<u>The more I learn, the more exciting</u> the world becomes.	When I learn more, the world <u>becomes more exciting</u>.

*Changed portions are underlined.

<u>Item Review and Revision</u>

Initial item review usually involves examination of the items from at least three perspectives: that of a technical specialist who is expert in the principles of measurement, a subject-matter specialist who can verify the appropriateness of the content, and an editorial specialist who can judge the appropriateness of the format and can point out grammatical and semantic problems (Tinkelman, 1971). Technical and editorial review of the SDLRS was performed; review in the subject matter area was not deemed necessary, since the content of the scale was selected based on the outcome of the national survey of experts on self-direction in learning. Review by a teacher of ESOL classes was also included, in light of the concern for removing idioms and minimizing difficult sentence structures. Four items were altered slightly to insure clarity of expression and understanding by the respondents. The sample item was also revised. Two of the revisions were suggested by both the native ABE students and the ESOL students. The remaining three were mentioned only by the ESOL students.

Assembly of the Scale
In the assembly of the scale, careful attention was given to clarity of instructions in order to ensure that the respondents would understand what they were being asked to do and to ensure that their responses would be recorded correctly. The instructions also clearly state that there are no right or wrong answers, in order to reduce anxiety and encourage thoughtful response (Henrysson, 1971, p. 133).

The instructions do not include specific reference to the purpose of the instrument. It is described as a questionnaire on learning preferences and attitudes toward learning. Fiske warns that the instructions for a self-report test which involves personality should not inform the subject of what is being measured (1971, p. 79). The lack of specificity concerning the purpose of the scale also constituted an effort to avoid one of the response sets warned against by Thorndike and Hagen--the tendency to respond with what is thought to be the desired response (1969, p. 393). As Thorndike and Hagen state, self-report inventories can be faked (1969, p. 395); subject ignorance of the actual purpose of the instrument and the statement that there are no right or wrong answers were designed to reduce the impulse to answer "as expected."

As was previously described, some of the items were stated in reverse form to offset the tendency to make all items on one end of the response continuum, either high or low. In the reversed items, the responses "I feel like this all the time," or, "I usually feel like this," indicate low self-direction. In the positively stated items, these responses indicate high self-direction. Avoidance of a pattern in the items was also planned. Placement of the reversed items was checked to ensure that there was no discernible pattern of high-response, high self-direction items and high-response, low self-direction items.

Possible responses to the items are listed in the instructions and reprinted at the top of each page of items to facilitate reference to them whenever necessary. Subjects are asked to choose the response option which best expresses their feelings. A sample item is provided.

Pre-tryout
The pre-tryout consisted of administration of the scale of 10 native-English speaking ABE students and 10 non-native- English speaking students in an intermediate level ESOL class. The pre-tryout respondents were not aware of the purpose of the scale. With both groups, the researcher explained that this was a tryout and asked the respondents to mark any items that were hard to read or understand. When the native students completed their responses the researcher

asked that they point out any items that were difficult to read or understand. With the ESOL students, the researcher went over the instrument item by item after the group had responded to it individually, reading the item and asking if there were any problems with it. The respondents' comments are summarized in Appendix A. All comments were carefully considered, and the items creating difficulty were reworded with the assistance of the tryout group. The reliability estimate for the pre-tryout was .80 (Cronbach's alpha).

<u>Tryout of The Instrument</u>
Cluster sampling will be used in the tryout of the SDLRA - ABE. The instrument will be administered to adults reading between the fourth and eighth grade levels in ABE and GED classes in several different states. Procedures for administration will be standardized, and subjects will respond during regular class periods. They will be allowed to take as much time as needed to complete the instrument.

<u>Analysis of Results</u>
Item analysis will be accomplished using the Statistical Package for the Social Sciences (SPSS). All items will be reviewed and will be revised or dropped from the scale. Primary criteria for choosing an item for revision will be item-text correlation and item difficulty. Based on the tryout data, the mean, range, standard deviation, and reliability estimate will be calculated.

SUMMARY

An adult basic education form of the Self-Directed Learning Readiness Scale (SDLRS-ABE) was developed to provide a more appropriate instrument for adults of low educational attainment and non-native speakers of English. The Delphi survey which formed the basis for the original scale also served as the basis for the SDLRS-ABE. Items were written in simple language, avoiding idioms, difficult grammar structures, and words less commonly used. After initial review and revision, the items were assembled. Further changes were made after a pre-tryout, involving 20 subjects, 10 native speakers and 10 non-native speakers.

After a multi-state tryout of the instrument, the results will be subjected to item analysis and the final version will be produced based on the results of that analysis.

Development of this form of the SDLRS is an effort to provide a more appropriate instrument for assessing readiness for self-direction in learning among adults of low educational attainment.

Appendix A: Pre-tryout Comments

Affirmations	F	Suggested Improvements F
1. "Good Test"	1	*1. I call it chocolate syrup, not 4 not chocolate sauce."
2. "Easy to understand	3	2. Item 15 - unclear
		3. Item 21 - unclear
3. "I like to have as much time as I need"	1	4. Item 34 - unclear
4. "It made me think.	1	

Changes

The sample item was reworded to read, "I like chocolate." Items 15, 21, 34, and 57 were reworded with the assistance of the tryout group.

*–Items 1 and 5 were mentioned both by the native ABE students and the ESOL students. The remaining items were mentioned only by the ESOL students.

REFERENCES

Brockett, R. G. (1983). Self-directed learning and the hard-to-reach adult, Lifelong Learning, 6, 16-18.

Brockett, R. G. (1985). Methodological and substantive issues in the measurement of self-directed learning readiness. Adult Education Quarterly, 36, 15-24.

Brookfield, S. (1984) Self-directed adult learning: A critical paradigm. Adult Education Quarterly, 35, 59-71.

Cronbach, L. J. (1951). Coefficient alpha and the internal structure of tests. Psychometrika, 16, 297-334.

Cronbach, L. J. (1971). Test Validation. In R. L. Thorndike (Ed.), Educational measurement (2nd ed). Washington, D.C.: American Council on Education.

Finestone, P. (1984). A construct validating of self-directed learning readiness scale with labour education participants. Doctoral dissertation. Toronto: University of Toronto.

Fiske, D. W. (1971). Measuring the concepts of personality. Chicago: Aldine.

Guglielmino, L. M. (1973). Development of the Self-Directed Learning Readiness Scale (doctoral dissertation, University of Georgia, 1977). Dissertation Abstracts International, 38, 6467 A.

Guglielmino, L. M. (1985). Florida's adult education ESOL staff development project: Final report. Unpublished manuscript.

Henrysson, S. (1971). Gathering, analyzing and using data on test items. In R. L. Thorndike (Ed.), Educational measurement (2nd ed.). Washington, D.C.: American Council on Education.

Leean C., & Sisco, B. (1981). Learning projects and self- planned learning efforts among undereducated adults in rural Vermont - Final report. Washington, D.C.: National Institute of Education.

Long, H. (1986). Self-directed learning readiness: An item analysis of Guglielmino's scale. Unpublished manuscript.

Long, H. and Agyekum, S. (1983). Guglielmino's self-directed learning readiness scale: A validation study. Higher Education, 12, 77-87.

Long, H. and Agyekum, S. (1984). Teacher ratings in the validation of Guglielmino's self-directed learning readiness scale. Higher Education, 13, 709-715.

Naisbitt, J. & Aburdene, P. (1985). Reinventing the corporation. New York: Warner Books.

Sisco, B. (1982). Personal communication with R. Brockett, August 1982.

Thorndike, R. L. & Hagen, E. P. (1969). Measurement and Education (3rd ed.). New York: John Wiley and Sons, Inc.

Tinkelman, S. N. (1971). Planning the objective test. In. R. L. Thorndike (Ed.). Educational measurement (2nd ed.). Washington, D. C.: American Council on Education.

Wesman, G. (1971). Writing the test item. In R. L. Thorndike, (Ed.), Educational measurement (2nd ed.). Washington, D.C.: American Council on Education.

Chapter Six

SELF DIRECTED LEARNING AMONG CLINICAL LABORATORY SCIENTISTS: A CLOSER LOOK AT THE OCLI

Carol McCoy and Michael Langenbach

In today's society, most knowledge-based professions require their members to utilize some method of continuing learning. In recent years, the media have made the public more aware of flaws in the competency levels of some professionals. In an attempt to regain and/or maintain the public trust in the competency level of professionals, many licensing boards and professional organizations mandate continuing education. (Shimberg, 1978)

Clinical laboratory scientists (Medical Technologists) are a science-based profession. In a health care field, one's knowledge is rapidly outdated. For example, ten years ago, no clinical laboratory scientist had heard of recombinant DNA techniques, monoclonal antibodies or the HIV. Continuing learning is a necessity. Changes in testing, interpretive data, and clinical relevance require the laboratory scientists to stay current in the field. Although one certifying body (National Accrediting Agency for Medical Laboratory Personnel) requires participation in continuing education or re-examination for recertification, the professional organization (American Society for Medical Technology) does not require either for membership. Nevertheless, it is generally agreed in the professional literature of the medical technologists that some form of continuing learning is necessary for maintenance of competency.

Continuing learning needs are unique for each individual. Individual needs require an individualized approach to learning. Self-directed learning is an individualized approach to learning. Knox, Knowles and Tough have each described the self-directed learning process as one in which the learner identifies the learning needs, sets the learning goals, determines and selects the types of learning experiences, locates the learning resources and evaluates the learning outcomes. (Brookfield, 1986)

As a group professionals are credited as being the most self-directed learners. (Cross, 1981) If professionals are self-directed learners, mandating continuing education should not be necessary. It appears that some professionals are self-directed learners while others are not. Has the propensity for self-directed learning been encouraged or discouraged by mandating continuing education within the professions? What outside factors, if any, influence self-directed learning? This study investigated some variables that could be factors in promoting or inhibiting self-directed learning.

The trend has been to require continuing education for recertification and/or relicensure. Some states have legislation requiring a certain number of hours of continuing education in order to retain the license. There has been no documentation of studies that have demonstrated that competency has been improved as a result of either mandatory or voluntary continuing education. One reason for the lack of documentation is the lack of adequate methods of evaluation of the program and learning process. An effective method to evaluate if learning has occurred and if the individual applied the knowledge has not been implemented. Implementation would require more time and money than is now expended. Without documentation, assumptions made are that although maintenance of competency is not assured by continuing education, lack of any continuing education implies lack of competence.

Planners of adult education, specifically continuing professional education, typically follow a program planning model that was originally designed in the fifties by Ralph Tyler. Although Tyler's model originally was designed for K-12 schools, it has been applied to many adult education programs. (Brookfield, 1986) The Council on the Continuing Education Unit expects any program for which continuing education units are awarded to follow their criteria and guidelines. The guidelines are based on Tyler's model. (Turner, 1979)

The majority of continuing professional education activities are planned for a target group. They typically do not reflect the specific learning needs of any one individual. In other words, the self-directed learning approach has had limited application for continuing education activities sponsored by various professional groups. Couple the 'canned program' approach with mandated continuing education requirements and the results often are less than satisfactory for the self-directed learner. This could explain why some professionals choose not to participate in continuing professional education.

Although it has been suggested that mandatory continuing professional education and planned programs could diminish the desire for self-directed learning (Darkenwald & Merriam, 1982; Tucker, 1984) a review of the literature failed to reveal any empirical studies in this area. If an institution requires a professional to participate in educational activities that do not meet the learning needs or interests of the individual it may follow, as Cross (1981) suggests, that the motivation to learn will be diminished. Conversely, the institution that promotes a self-directed learning approach in which the individual selects the learning experiences most appropriate for job performance may foster an atmosphere of self-directed learning.

Oddi reviewed the literature on self-directed learning and noted that Brockett, Brookfield and Griffin all pointed out the lack of theoretical construct for self-directing learning. (Oddi, 1985) In her review, she searched for a theoretical framework for personality characteristics of the self-directed learner.

Oddi (1985) developed a 24 item instrument called the Oddi Continuing Learning Inventory (OCLI). In developing and validating the instrument she used graduate students in nursing, law, and adult education as her sample. Factor analysis was performed on the data. She identified three factors associated with self-directed continuing learning.

> Factor I   Ability to work independently and learn through the involvement of others.
> Factor II Ability to be self regulating
> Factor III Avidity for reading (Oddi, 1985)

The OCLI was the instrument used in this study. For the purpose of this research a royalty-free copyright license for the use of the instrument was granted by Lorys F. Oddi.

It is important that adult educators know if current methods of administering continuing professional education diminish the self-directed learning tendencies among professionals and if these methods contribute to non-participation by some professionals. Does the work environment promote or deter self-directed learning tendencies among professionals?

METHOD

Clinical laboratory scientists employed in five different laboratories in a metropolitan area of a Southwestern state were the subjects for this study. The laboratories represented a range of expectations regarding mandated continuing professional education, i.e., one or two were considered low on the scale requirements and provisions for continuing professional education, and the others were considered high. All clinical laboratory scientists in the five institutions were invited to participate. The Oddi Continuing Learning Inventory was administered to them. At the same time the subjects were given the OCLI, they were also given a personal questionnaire that was designed to elicit responses to organizational questions regarding mandatory continuing professional education, their continuing learning habits, as well as demographic questions. Three hundred and seventy-two questionnaires and inventories were administered and one hundred and sixty-nine (45%) usable protocols were returned. Respondents were placed in groups based upon how they categorized the continuing education climate of their institutions. The emerging categories were:

GROUP I: MANDATORY CONTINUING EDUCATION

Continuing education was required of the employees; it was provided by the institution in-house and participation in educational activities outside the institution was encouraged by paid time off and/or financial support of continuing education activity. n=103

GROUP II: CONTINUING EDUCATION NOT MANDATED BUT ENCOURAGED

Continuing education was not required of the employees; there were occasional continuing education sessions provided by the institution and participation in educa -tional activities outside the institution was encouraged by paid time off and/or financial support of continuing education activity. n=29

GROUP III: CONTINUING EDUCATION NOT MANDATED AND NOT ENCOURAGED

Continuing education was not required of the employees; little or no continuing education was offered by the institution and participation in educational activities outside the institution was not encouraged, i.e., no paid time off and no financial support. n=37

An Analysis of Variance (ANOVA) was used to determine if there were significant differences in the group means of the OCLI scores in the organizations with differently perceived requirements regarding continuing professional education. The OCLI scores also were correlated (Pearson's Correlation Coefficient) with items from the personal questionnaire that could be treated as measurement data (twenty-nine items). For yes/no responses, the Chi Square statistic was used to determine if proportions of yes responses differed among the three groups. An analysis by Oddi's three factors was performed to determine if any of them would reveal differences. Finally a factor analysis was conducted to see if this administration of the inventory yielded the same three factors Oddi found.

RESULTS

Reliability of the OCLI was estimated with Cronbach's Alpha. The reliability was .79, sufficiently high for the purpose of the study.

The overall mean score of the Oddi Continuing Learning Inventory (OCLI) given to the clinical laboratory scientists in the various organizational settings was expected to be relatively high. The high score would be an indication of self-directed continuing learners. The high means obtained by the students in Oddi's study led her to believe that her sample might include a large number of self-directed continuing learners. Comparison of the means of the student groups studies by Oddi and the subjects in this study is seen in Table 6.1.

Table 6.1: A Comparison of OCLI Means: CLS and Oddi's Group

GROUP	N	Mean	S.D.
Clinical Lab Scientists	169	129.1	15.9
Nursing Students	78	128.2	
Adult Educ. Students	83	125.4	19.03*
Law Students	110	119.0	

*Standard Deviation of Oddi's total groups.

It was expected that those who perceived mandated continuing education from their institutions would demonstrate a lower OCLI score than those who did not perceive a mandated continuing education, i.e., that Group I scores would be lower than Group II and III. This was not the case. Table 6.2 contains the mean and standard deviation of each of the three groups.

Table 6.2: OCLI Scores of CLS in Three Differently Perceived Organizational Settings

GROUP	N	MEAN	S.D.	HI	LO
I	103	128.7	16.0	160	46
II	29	131.5	13.9	156	101
III	37	128.0	16.3	161	65

Group I: Continuing Education Required and Encouraged

Group II: Continuing Education Not Required But Encouraged

Group III: Continuing Education Not Required an Not Encouraged.

A one-way Analysis of Variance was performed on the OCLI scores. The overall mean of the one hundred and sixty-nine clinical laboratory scientists was 129.1. The difference among the means of the three groups was not significant, $F=0.44$, $p>.05$. The ANOVA results are summarized in Table 6.3.

Table 6.3: Analysis of Variance of OCLI Scores of Three Groups

SOURCE	DF	SUM OF SQUARES	MEAN SQUARES	F VALUE
Groups	2	221.55	110.77	1[*]
Error	166	41578.93	250.47	

*non-significant

Additional review of the OCLI scores of each group failed to elucidate any distinguishing characteristics. The means and standard deviations were so similar that it appeared the groups were homogeneous. Overall the data from the personal questionnaire revealed that, as a group, the majority of learning activities engaged in by the subjects were self-directed.

The most frequently cited learning activities were reading journals and books. The OCLI scores obtained by the clinical laboratory scientists were indicative of self-directed learners. However, the personal questionnaire revealed that the number of learning activities in which subjects engaged, did not correspond to their OCLI scores.

Analysis of the variables in the personal questionnaire failed to identify any variable that was strongly associated with the OCLI scores. There were two statistically significant findings though small in magnitude ($<.30$) when Pearson's correlation Coefficient was applied to the data. There was a negative correlation between the OCLI scores and the degree year (-0.27, $p=.004$) and a positive correlation between OCLI scores and reading professional journals (0.27, $p=.0005$). However the distribution of the number of professional journals read was highly skewed to the right.

For the Yes/No response in the questionnaire, the Chi Square statistic was used to determine if the proportion of yes responses differed among the three groups. Of the fourteen yes/no items, four were statistically significant at a $p<.01$. level. Three of the four differences served to validate the original classification of the three groups. The four items were the perceived lack of support from the supervisor in the employees' continuing education interests and goals; the feeling of inadequacy to meet the future directions of the clinical laboratory sciences; the failure to participate in continuing education because of cost; and failure to participate in continuing education for other reasons not listed in the questionnaire, i.e., "none" category. Table 6.4 summarizes the findings.

Table 6.4: Percent of Subjects Within Each Group Answering
Yes on Selected* Yes/No Questions

Variable	Group I	Group II	Group III
Support of CE from superior	89.7	85.7	48.4
Equipped for future directions of profession	88.8	71.4	57.6
Nonparticipation in CE due to cost	22.3	20.7	56.8
Nonparticipation in CE "none"	14.6	41.4	35.1

Group I: Continuing Education Required and Encouraged
Group II: Continuing Education Not Required But Encouraged.
Group III: Continuing Education Not Required and Not Encouraged

*only questions for which Chi Square was significant (p < .01)

The OCLI was made up of three factors (Oddi, 1985). All of the comparisons originally conducted over the total OCLI scores were repeated separately with each of the original factors. The results were the same: no differences among the three groups when using ANOVA and only moderate relationships to years since degree (.30 with factor 1) and professional journals read (.29 with factor 3).

In the present study the sample size was only 169 and not really adequate for a valid factor analysis, if we apply the rule of ten subjects per item. However, a factor analysis was performed to see if the results matched those of Oddi's. Given the precautions of a smaller than necessary sample, the most interpretable analysis was a four factor solution. One of the factors had a close correspondence with Oddi's factor II, "Ability to be self-regulating". Four of the five items she had for this factor loaded on one of our four. The correspondence ended there, however, as the other three obtained factors bore little resemblance to her other two and seven of the twenty-four items either loaded on more than one factor or did not load at all.

CONCLUSIONS AND DISCUSSION

The purpose of this study was to investigate if there were differences in self-directing learning and participation in continuing education in different organizational settings. The assumption was made that clinical laboratory scientists in an organizational environment of planned, programmed, and mandated continuing education would demonstrate less self-directedness in learning than clinical laboratory scientists working in organizational settings that did not impose continuing education requirements. The findings in the study failed to reveal organizational barriers to the tendency to self-directed learning.

Based upon the OCLI scores, the study indicated that clinical laboratory scientists possess personality characteristics associated with self-directed learners.

The statistically significant, low magnitude (-.27) finding with degree year and OCLI scores is open for speculation. Are the individuals who entered the clinical laboratory science profession several years ago self-directed learners while the newer professionals fail to possess those self-directed learning personality characteristics? Do the older clinical laboratory science professionals have more free time to devote to learning activities? Do the older clinical laboratory science professionals feel the need to update their knowledge in an attempt to stay current while the younger professionals do not perceive this necessity since their knowledge is newly acquired? One must also ask if the concept of professionalism and the need for continuing learning is emphasized in the preservice curriculum.

The OCLI scores and demographic variables were not seen to identify and/or distinguish one group from the others. In fact the only meaningful correlation between learning activity items and the OCLI scores was the reading of professional journals. One could question if the OCLI provides a valid measurement of self-directed continuing learning. At least it appears to have failed to demonstrate concurrent validity in this study. It is also possible that there is a need for additional items in the OCLI that would provide a more thorough definition of the self-directed learner.

If one assumes the OCLI measures self-directed continuing learning then one must ask why there was a lack of correlation between the scores and learning activities cited by the subjects in this study. One must also ask why there were no significant differences in the groups that had mandated continuing education imposed upon them compared with the groups that did not have mandated these requirements. It could be that mandated continuing education does not diminish the tendency toward self-directed learning. The apparent homogeneity of all the groups could be explained if mandated continuing education does not deter self-directed learning tendencies.

For clinical laboratory scientists, the factor analysis identified one stable factor that compared very well with one of Oddi's factors:

Factor II (ability to be self-regulating). The ability to be self-regulating is a characteristic that must be possessed by clinical laboratory scientists as well as many other professionals. There is no readily available answer for the lack of factor correspondence of clinical laboratory scientists and the groups in Oddi's study. It appears the strength of the OCLI, for clinical laboratory scientists, lies with the items related to being self-regulating.

REFERENCES

Apps, J. (1979). Problems in Continuing Education. New York, McGraw-Hill in C. Day & H. Baskett (1982). Discrepancies Between Intentions and Practice. Reexamining some Basic Assumptions about Adult and Continuing Professional Education International Journal of Lifelong Education. 1 (2). 143-155.

Armstrong, D. (1971). Adult Learners of Low Educational Attainment. The Self-Concept, Backgrounds and Educative Behavior of Average and High Learning Adults of Low Educational Attainment. Unpublished doctoral dissertation. University of Toronto.

Brockett, R. & Hiemstra, R. (1985). Bridging the Theory-Practice Gap in Self-directed Learning, in S. Brookfield Self-Directed Learning from Theory to Practice (theme). New Directions for Continuing Education. March 25, 6-16.

Brookfield, S. (1986). Understanding and Facilitating Adult Learning. San Francisco: Jossey-Bass.

Cross, K. (1981). Adults as Learners. San Francisco: Jossey-Bass.

Darkenwald, G. & Merriam, S. (1982). Adult Education: Foundations of Practice. New York: Harper & Row.

Oddi, L. (1985). Development of an Instrument to Identify Self-directed Continuing Learners. Adult Education Quarterly. Winter 36:(2). 97-107.

Shimberg, B. (1978, September). Continuing Education Records. Can They Withstand the Scrutiny? Paper presented at the National Invitational Conference on Continuing Education for Allied Health Professions, Chicago, IL.

Tucker, B. & Huerta, C. (1984). Continuing Professional Education. (ED 252674).

Turner, W. (1979). Criteria and Guidelines for the Use of the Continuing Education Unit. Council on CEU. Silver Springs, MD.

Chapter Seven

A META-ANALYTIC STUDY OF THE RELATIONSHIP BETWEEN ADULT SELF-DIRECTION IN LEARNING AND PSYCHOLOGICAL WELL-BEING: A REVIEW OF THE RESEARCH FROM 1977 TO 1987

Sandra K. McCune and Gonzalo Garcia, Jr.

Many adults decide on their own to become involved in educational activities (Penland, 1979; Tough, 1971). The term self-directed learning has been used to describe these self-initiated educational endeavors (Caffarella & O'Donnell, 1987). One might then characterize the adult engaged in self-directed learning as demonstrating adult self-direction in learning. For the purposes of this study adult self-direction in learning is defined as a set of skills, abilities, attitudes, or personality characteristics of an adult that facilitate involvement in self-directed learning activities (adapted from Guglielmino, 1978; Oddi, 1984; Skager, 1984).

In the past decade there has accumulated a body of research investigating the relationship of adult self-direction in learning to various psychosocial variables (Caffarella & O'Donnell, 1987). Within these studies there is a subset that suggests a relationship between adult self-direction in learning and psychological well-being, where psychological well-being is taken to mean a global construct incorporating such concepts as self-esteem, creativity, perceived health, and life satisfaction among others. This conceptualization of psychological well-being is based on Jahoda's (1958) classical review of the nature of psychological health. She summarized six major conceptualizations of psychological health:

1. Attitudes toward oneself (e.g., self-concept, self-esteem, self-respect, self-acceptance).

2. Growth, development, and self-actualization (e.g., creativity, spontaneity, openness to change and learning, acceptance of others).

3. Balance of personality (e.g., resilience, flexibility, tolerance of risk).

4. Inner-directedness (e.g., autonomy, independence).

5. Realistic view of world (e.g., correct perception of self, correct perception of others).

6. Successful mastery of environment (e.g., competence in work, adequacy in social interactions, ability to solve problems, life-satisfaction).

Reviews of self-directed learning have been written (Brookfield, 1984; Cafferella & O'Donnell, 1987; Mocker & Spear, 1982) but none have addressed, specifically, the relationship between adult self-direction in learning and psychological well-being.

Glass (1976) has suggested a procedure for statistical review of research results which he calls meta-analysis. Meta-analysis has been used to examine pretest sensitization effects (Willson & Puttnam, 1982), to examine the effect of class size (Glass & Smith, 1979), and to examine the relationship between educational expenditures and study achievement (Childs & Shakeshaft, 1986). In each of these studies the use of meta-analysis allowed for a precise examination of the variables under study and their interrelationships.

In a meta-analysis the statistic reported for a study result serves as the dependent variable and is called the "effect size." For the present study each individual correlation coefficient relating self-direction to psychological well-being was recorded as an effect size. The effect size became the unit of analysis for the study. Independent variables for the meta-analysis are relevant study characteristics including publication year, publication form, study location, mean age of the subjects, study quality, and the like. These characteristics are assigned numerical values so that descriptive statistics can be compiled and statistical analyses to examine relationships between these variables can be performed.

Using the procedure of meta-analysis, the purposes of this study were to synthesize existing studies to (a) investigate the strength of the relationship between adult self-direction in learning and psychological well-being and (b) examine to what extent the strength of this relationship is influenced by other variables.

METHOD

Population
The population of interest for this study was the full set of existing studies on adult self-direction in learning from 1977 to 1987 which met the following criteria:

1. The study was written in English or an English translation was obtainable.

2. The concept of self-direction in learning was operationally defined in a manner consistent with the definition formulated for the present study.

3.   The subjects in the study were at least sixteen years of age.

4.   The study reported quantitative results from which a correlation coefficient could be obtained or meaningfully estimated.

<u>Sampling Procedure</u>

Every effort was made to acquire all published and unpublished studies that met the criteria. Computer retrieval searches were conducted from the following databases: Educational Resources Information Center (ERIC), Dissertation Abstracts, Nursing and Allied Health Literature (NAHL), MEDLARS produced by the National Library of Medicine, PsycLIT which is compiled from material published in <u>Psychological Abstracts</u> and the PsychINFO database (produced by the American Psychological Association), and Social Science Citation Index. Manual searches of the Resources in Education (RIE), Current Index to Journals in Education (CIJE), and Dissertation Abstracts International (DAI) were also conducted. Furthermore, all bibliographic references of retrieved studies were examined to identify further studies that might be included. Finally, authors of studies were contacted to request suggestions as to the location of additional studies.

Descriptor terms used were "independent study," "self-direction in learning," "self-directedness," "self-directed learning," "self-directed learning readiness," "lifelong learning," "continuing education," "correspondence study," "self-study," "autodidactic learning," "distance education," "self-instruction," "self-planned learning," "learning projects," "self-education," and "self-teaching." To limit the number of irrelevant citations that might be retrieved, the descriptors "adult" and "research" were adjoined to the previous lists. The years searched were from 1977 to 1987.

Hundreds of studies were rejected on the basis of the abstract. Most of the remaining studies were dissertations which had to be ordered through interlibrary loan or purchased. The authors purchased dissertation copies from University Microfilms International, the University of Chicago, and the National Library of Canada. The studies were read and some were dismissed as not meeting the criteria for inclusion. Studies were found to be not usable if (1) no statistics were reported; (2) reported statistics were not sufficient for calculating or estimating an effect size; (3) the subjects were not adults as defined by the authors of this study; or (4) the concept of self-direction in learning was not congruent with the definition of self-direction in learning formulated for this study. When the same research was found in more than one form, such as dissertation and journal, the study with more extensive report was used and the other(s) discarded.

Despite efforts to exhaust the population the authors were unable to acquire all the studies because some studies were unobtainable by the deadline for proceeding with subsequent steps in the meta-analysis. It was felt that the remaining sample of studies was an adequate representation of the research.

Variables

A coding form was developed so that effect sizes and study characteristics could be recorded. The coding form was pilot tested on several studies that had been dismissed from the analysis (the subjects of these studies were not adults).

Besides effect size (dependent variable), other coded study characteristics (independent variables) were: (1) sign of effect size; (2) type of statistic from which the effect size was determined; (3) retrieval source of document; (4) publication year; (5) publication form; (6) geographic location of the study within 11 regions (see Table 7.1); (7) discipline of principal investigator; (8) sex of principal investigator; (9) involvement of principal investigator; (10) sample size; (11) mean age of the subjects; (12) how mean age value was obtained; (13) percent of females in the sample; (14) how percent female was obtained; (15) whether the study had (a) less than 25% white, (b) 25%-75% white, or (c) more than 75% white; (16) how the choice of percent white was determined; (17) mean educational attainment level; (18) how mean educational attainment level obtained; (19) whether median socioeconomic status was (a) low (below $10,000), (b) medium, or (c) high (above $50,000); (20) student status of subjects; (22) instrument used to measure self-direction in learning; and (23) study quality on a scale from one to three (based on seven criteria suggested by Hembree (1984).

Method of Analysis

Each correlation coefficient and the 23 coded independent variables were entered into various statistical procedures using the SPSSx (1986) statistical package. Descriptive statistics and analysis of variance were the major statistical techniques used to describe the studies and characterize the correlation between self-direction in learning and psychological well-being.

Table 7.1: Convention for Assigning Areas to Geographic Regions

---

Geographic Regions_____States_____

United States

New England	Connecticut, Maine, Massachusetts, New Hampshire, Rhode Island, Vermont
Atlantic Coastal	Delaware, Maryland, New York, New Jersey, Pennsylvania
South Atlantic	Florida, Georgia, North Carolina, South Carolina, Virginia, West Virginia
South Central	Alabama, Arkansas, Kentucky, Louisiana, Mississippi, Oklahoma Tennessee, Texas
North Central	Illinois, Indiana, Iowa, Kansas, Michigan, Minnesota, Missouri, Nebraska, North Dakota, Ohio, South Dakota, Wisconsin
Western Mountain	Arizona, Colorado, Idaho, Montana New Mexico, Nevada, Utah, Wyoming
Pacific	California, Oregon, Washington
Alaska	
Hawaii	

Canada

Limitations
The findings of this study are subject to the following limitations:

1. The authors established criteria to determine which studies would be used in the analysis. Therefore, the findings are limited to those studies which met the criteria.

2. Some research statistics had to be estimated. Although this procedure decreases the reliability of the findings, this strategy is preferable to eliminating studies from the meta-analysis (Hunter, Schmidt, & Jackson, 1982).

3. The scope of this study does not allow for the determination of interactions that may exist between variables.

4. The nature of correlational research does not allow for determining a causative relationship.

RESULTS

The Studies
A total of 28 studies[*] was located which had usable statistics. The studies represented a total of 5653 subjects with a mean sample size of 201.9 for all studies. The studies ranged in size from 34 subjects to 1501 subjects with the median study size falling at 110 subjects. The mean age of the subjects for the 216 studies from which this statistic was obtainable or estimable ranged from 17 up to 78.4 years. The overall mean age of the subjects was 40.2 years. For the 26 studies that reported information on the sex of the subjects, the mean percent of female students was 64.9%. There was one all male study and two all female studies. For the 11 studies for which ethnicity could be determined, the typical study had a majority of white subjects. Twenty-seven studies provided sufficient data for determining mean educational achievement level which ranged from 6 to 20 years of schooling. The overall mean educational achievement level was 14.2 years. Information about socioeconomic status was provided in 17 studies indicating that the average subject was middle-class. Thirteen of the studies used students as subjects. The mean study quality was 2.35, ranging from a low of 1.67 to a high of 2.89. Guglielmino's (1978) Self-Directed Learning Readiness Scale was used as the instrument for mesuring self-direction in learning in 18 of the studies. Tough's interview schedule was used for this purpose in four of the studies. Other instruments or methods were used infrequently.

---

[*]A list of the studies is available from the authors at the Department of Mathematics and Statistics, Stephen F. Austin State University, Nacogdoches, TX 75962.

The sex of the principal investigator was female in 60.7% of the studies, male in 35.7%, and not specified in one study.

Additional descriptive information about the studies by location is reported in Table 7.2; by publication year in Table 7.3; by publication form in Table 7.4; by discipline of investigator in Table 7.5; and by involvement of investigator in Table 7.6.

Discussion

The results indicate that research investigating the relationship between adult self-direction in learning and psychological well-being has focused on white, middle class subjects. Furthermore, the 28 studies examined here suggest that the subjects are mostly female, middle-aged students with about 14 years of schooling.

Table 7.2: Distribution of Studies by Location

Region	Number of Studies	%
New England	2	7.1
Atlantic Coastal States	6	21.4
South Atlantic States	8	28.6
South Central States	2	7.1
North Central States	8	28.6
Canada	1	3.6
United States (generally)	1	3.6

In addition, these studies indicate that the typical principal investigator is a female outside investigator who is an adult educator. Her instrument of choice for measuring adult self-directedness in learning is Guglielmino's (1978) Self-Directed Learning Readiness Scale. More studies have been done in the North Central and South Atlantic states with 1985 being the peak year for number of studies performed. The overall quality of studies has been good.

The Effects

A total of 90 effect sizes were obtained from the 28 studies. The mean for all effect sizes was .24 (S.D. = .203). Seventy-nine percent of the effect sizes were positive. Also,

Table 7.3: Distribution of Studies by Publication Year

Year	Number of Studies	%
77	1	3.6
78	3	10.7
79	2	7.1
80	1	3.6
81	3	10.7
82	2	7.1
83	3	10.7
84	2	7.1
85	8	28.6
86	2	7.1
87	1	3.6

Table 7.4: Distribution of Studies by Publication Form

Form	Number of Studies	%
Journal	9	32.1
Dissertation	18	63.3
Book	1	3.6

Table 7.5: Distribution of Studies by Discipline of Investigator

Form	Number of Studies	%
Adult Education	16	57.1
Education Psychololgy	3	10.7
Other Education	1	3.6
Nursing	6	21.4
Sociology	1	3.6
Library Science	1	3.6

Table 7.6: Distribution of Studies by Involvement of Investigator

Involvement	Number of Studies	%
Outside Investigator	25	89.3
Teacher	2	7.1
Administrator	1	3.6

67.9% of the effect sizes were reported as either a Pearson's Product-Moment correlation coefficient, a Spearman's rho, or Cramer's phi, 10.7% of the effect sizes were determined from a reported t statistic, 3.6% of the effect sizes were calculated from a chi-square statistic or a 2x2 contingency table, and 17.8% of the effect sizes were estimated from other reported statistics.

There was no statistically significant (= .05) correlation between effect size (ES) and publication form, location of study, discipline of investigator, involvement of the investigator, sex of the principal investigator, mean age of the subjects, percent female subjects, percent white subjects, mean educational attainment level of subjects, median socioeconomic status of the subjects, student status of subjects, location of the study or instrument used to measure self-direction in learning (SDL). Publication year (p < .01), sample size (p < .05), and study quality (p < .01) were significantly related to effect size.

A t-test between studies of questionable quality (quality score more than two standard deviations below the mean) and the remaining studies failed to find a difference in the average effect between the two groups; therefore, the lower quality studies were not omitted from the analysis.

Discussion
Cohen (1977) has suggested that an effect size (when using correlation as a measure of effect size) of magnitude .100 - .242 is small, one between .243 and .370 is medium, and one .371 or greater is large. He commented that these values could serve as guidelines; but one should also be aware that effects sought on psychosocial variables are likely to be small "...because of the attenuation in validity of the measures employed and the subtlety of the issue frequently involved" (p.13). Thus, the overall effect size of .24 for the study, though it falls in the low category of Cohen's labels, might be called moderate.

An interesting finding in the self-direction in learning-psychological well-being relation is the decline in the magnitude of the relationship over time. Earlier studies reported a stronger relationship than later studies.

The finding that the relationship between adult self-directedness in learning and psychological well-being is associated with the sample size is due to the very large nationwide survey of 1501 subjects by Patrick Penland (1977).

The issue of study quality is one that cannot be taken lightly. Since the strength of the association between adult self-direction in learning and psychological well-being was found to be related to the study quality, the authors had to further investigate this variable. Since, no difference between poor studies and good studies were found, study quality did not bias the findings.

From the results of this meta-analysis it appears that self-direction learning and psychological well-being show a relationship. Although, one should not conclude that self-direction in learning causes psychological well-being, those working with adults should be encouraged to provide rich and diverse learning opportunities. By so doing educators may be contributing to the psychological well-being of the adult population. Furthermore, adult educators should consider the inverse possibility: that psychological well-being may be necessary before self-directed learning activities are desired or undertaken. Along with providing programs, there may be a need to assist adults in achieving psychological well-being so that they can become effective self-initiated learners. Counseling and support systems may help in this endeavor.

REFERENCES

Brookfield, S. (1984). Self-directed learning: A critical paradigm. Adult Education Quarterly, 36, 15-24.

Caffarella, R., & O'Donnell, J. (1987). Self-directed adult learning: A critical paradigm revisited. Adult Education Quarterly, 37, 199-221.

Cohen, J. (1977). Statistical power analysis for the behavior sciences (rev. ed.). New York: Academic Press.

Glass, G. (1976). Primary, secondary, and meta-analysis of research. Educational Researcher, 5, 3-8.

Guglielmino, L. (1978). Development of the self-directed learning readiness scale (Doctoral dissertation, University of Georgia, 1977). Dissertation Abstracts International, 38, 6467A.

Hunter, J., Schmidt, F., & Jackson, G. (1982). Meta-analysis: cumulating research findings across studies. Beverly Hills, CA: Sage.

Hembree, R. (1984). Model for meta-analysis of research in education with a demonstration in mathematics education: Effects of hand-held calculators (Doctoral dissertation, University of Tennessee, 1984). Dissertation Abstracts International, 45, 10A.

Jahoda, M. (1958). Current concepts of positive mental health. New York: Basic Books, Inc.

Mocker, D. & Spear, G. (1982). Lifelong learning: Formal, nonformal, and self-directed. Columbus, OH: National Center for Research in Vocational Education, The Ohio State University. (ERIC Document Reproduction Service No. ED 220 723)

Oddi, L. (1984). Development of an instrument to measure self-directed continuing learning (Doctoral dissertation, Northern Illinois University). Dissertation Abstracts International, 46, 49A.

Penland, P. (1977). Self-planned learning in America. Final report. Washington, D.C.: National Center for Educational Statistics.

Penland, P. (1979). Self-initiated learning. Adult Education, 29, 170-179.

Skager, R. (1984). Organizing schools to encourage self-direction in learners. New York: Pergamon Press.

SPSSX Inc. (1986). SPSSX User's Guide. New York: McGraw-Hill.

Tough, A. (1971). The adult's learning project: A fresh approach to theory and practice in adult learning. Toronto: Ontario Institute for Studies in Education.

A Meta-Analytic Study

Chapter Eight

BRIDGING THEORY AND PRACTICE: APPLICATIONS IN THE DEVELOPMENT OF SERVICES FOR SELF-DIRECTED LEARNERS

Judith Klippel DeJoy and Helen Mills

Self-directed learning phenomena continue to attract significant attention within the field of adult education; research efforts have explored the frequency, characteristics, and theoretical underpinnings of adult self-directed learning while practitioners have experimented with applications of the concept both inside and outside the adult classroom.

Extensive reviews of research on the nature of self-directed learning in adults (Caffarella & O'Donnell, 1987) support the validity of the phenomena and the legitimacy of continued efforts to apply self-directed learning concepts in educational settings. Certainly, further work is required to extract a fundamental understanding of self-directed learning from the several different explanations available. The extent to which self-directed learning is a semi-formal planning process (Tough, 1979), a creative response to particular circumstances (Spear & Mocker, 1984), or a non-linear process of activity and reflection (Brookfield, 1986; Danis & Tremblay, 1987) is not determined. The theme common to these different explanations lies in the concept of control of the learning process by the learner.

The increasing use of self-directed learning programs or strategies is related to the pace of today's "information society"; there is a growing appreciation of the new demands on working adults to continually learn, and re-learn, when faced with rapidly changing information bases and new technology. The challenge of remaining competent on the job is bigger, and more complex, than ever, and the growing population of older workers and retired adults adds to the renewed attention focused on informal, or self-directed, adult learning.

The stage is set for implementation of the concepts of the self-directed learning process, not in the controlled environment of research study, but in adult learning environments where learners participate in activities to meet their educational needs and satisfy their interests throughout their working and personal lives.

In this paper, we direct attention to an ongoing educational program which is based on several elements of self-directed learning phenomena and offers a range of services to a selected variety of adult learners. The application of theoretical concepts to the development and implementation of the Learning Lab will be described, as well as what has been learned about the self-directed learner in a continuing education context.

APPLICATIONS OF THEORY TO PROGRAM DESIGN

The Georgia Center for Continuing Education is a major continuing education facility operating within the context of a land-grant state higher education institution. The Georgia Center opened in 1957 under the auspices of a W. K. Kellogg Foundation grant. Serving working professional adults predominantly interested in non-credit continuing education opportunities, the Georgia Center offers service to some 90,000 adult learners annually, with about 35,000 of these adults attending conference activities at the Center itself. This population of adult learners is drawn from across the country and across the state. In addition, the resident academic population and the local community surrounding the University make use of the Center. Other learners are served through an extensive off-campus program throughout the state.

In 1984, a Kellogg Foundation grant was awarded to the University for application in four major areas; one of these areas covered the Georgia Center and included the development of a self-directed learning lab for adults. The Personal Adult Learning Lab was created to provide a learning environment which could facilitate self-directed learning efforts by adults and explore the phenomena. With this mission in mind, goals for the Learning Lab were developed: 1) to facilitate the self-directed learning process through the use of on-site staff; 2) to provide a variety of self-directed instructional materials for individual use; 3) to provide a physical locale furnished with the necessary educational technology for delivering individualized instruction; 4) to extend the limitations of time and space by providing access to materials and other resources (such as content experts, bibliographic services, etc.) at a distance via communication technology; and 5) to observe and record the characteristics of adult Learning Lab users, their interests, choices, and evaluations of their particular self-directed learning experience.

In light of the overall mission, the design of the Learning Lab was guided by some of the fundamental concepts of self-directed learning in adult populations, as follows.

Design Elements
The design of the Learning Lab involved these elements: specific client populations, particular instructional materials, appropriate delivery modes, and the nature of the learning environment.

Client Populations. Knowles (1980) has freshly interpreted the adult learner as an individual: 1) moving towards independency or self-directedness; 2) who approaches learning with a rich experience; 3) who is more or less ready to learn, dependent on their developmental life stage; and 4) who is interested in immediate application and problem solving. In our effort to develop learning opportunities in line with these assumptions, the Learning Lab identified three categories of adult learners from the larger community: the working professionals attending GA Center conferences for continuing professional education, the academic faculty and staff, and adults in the surrounding city and county. The conferee population represented the primary client group. A survey was conducted of conferee learning interests to assess the types of learning needs existing among the conference participants.

Instructional Resources and Delivery Modes. The survey of conference participants conducted in 1984 suggested several generic content areas which would be helpful to a wide variety of professionals: management and communication skills, computer training, and career exploration.

In keeping with the concept of learner "control" of part or all of the self-directed experience (Brookfield, 1986; Tough, 1979; Knowles, 1980) all the instructional resources chosen for the Learning Lab were required to be self-instructional and self-paced.

In support of the self-directed learning process, the concept of individual learning style becomes important. Adults experience the learning process in different ways, as a function of any number of variables, such as previous experiences, levels of attainment, intelligence, motivation and age (Evan, 1987). Certain predilections for processing information, such as reading, listening, practicing, writing, etc. also contribute to the idiosyncratic nature of adult learning (Dixon, 1985; James & Galbraith, 1985; Korhonen & McCall, 1986). We can assume that these types of variables are at work during self-directed learning experiences.

Therefore, a variety of learning resources are currently available in the Learning Lab in several different delivery modes: computer-assisted instruction (CAI) packages, interactive video materials, videotapes, audiocassettes, self- assessment instruments, workbooks and manuals. The majority of the computer-assisted instruction material is made up of self-assessment inventories and practice components. Most programs produce hard-copy printouts summarizing individual responses, and workbooks accompany the programs. The workbooks serve not as interactive components but as reference resources. Interactive video training programs are available for self-directed computer training; in addition to an introductory-level program, instruction is available for several commonly-used application programs. This interactive video training workstation is made up of the interactive video player and monitor next to the computer with its operational software, so that the user can control the pace of the training program as he/she practices with the computer. A manual accompanying each training program provides periodic self- tests with feedback.

The operation of any delivery mode for self-instruction is a simple task; the CAI packages do not require users to already know how to operate a computer or how to type.

The Learning Environment. Tough (1979) and Knowles (1975) have described the elements of the self-directed planning process, and emphasized the learner's needs for materials, people, equipment, proper space and a conducive atmosphere in pursuing self-directed learning. These ideas guided the development of the Learning Lab's physical environment. Both the current space and the eventual large-scale facility were designed to promote a sense of privacy, provide for physical comfort during learning, and support ongoing learning events with the presence of a trained facilitator. Materials are readily accessible and self-instructional; equipment is easy to operate. The concept of "readiness" for self-directed learning (Brockett, 1985; Caffarella & Caffarella, 1986; Guglielmino, 1978) suggests the need for supporting the learner's efforts to identify appropriate materials by the interaction with someone who can help during information searches. In addition, it has been suggested that the "key" to self-directed learning lies in recognition by the learner of the value of what they already know (Hall, 1986); a skilled facilitator can contribute to this understanding on the part of the adult learner.

FULL-SCALE IMPLEMENTATION AND EVALUATION

The Conference Connection
The ultimate goal of the Learning Lab regarding on-site self-directed learning opportunities for adult professionals is to make what we call the conference CONNECTION. When a particular conference makes the Learning Lab part of its agenda, in some way, we identify this as a conference CONNECTION; several examples follow.

The first CONNECTION was made in November, 1986, when a conference group leader scheduled a self-assessment program on salesmanship for his conference participants. The program complemented the conference objectives, and many of the conferees who used the Lab returned on their own time.

The second such CONNECTION was made between a large conference of city and municipal clerks and the Learning Lab's supervisory skills materials. Time spent in the Lab earned certification credit towards the clerks' certification program, and special times were set aside for participants to use the Lab.

Throughout the past year, several conferences have used pre-conference mailings to inform their participants of the Learning Lab and permit pre-conference scheduling of appointments. Conferences added specific descriptions of the Lab to their conference brochures, and several included the Learning Lab as a concurrent session on their agenda. In several cases, specialized Learning Lab demonstrations have been part of the conference program.

There are a wide variety of ways to make a conference CONNECTION, ranging from reserving specific hours for unstructured conferee use to incorporating the Lab directly into the conference program, allowing participants to work independently and, subsequently, describe their assessment results in an organized group discussion.

Interests of the Self-Directed Learner

As revealed in Table 8.1, the largest percentage of conference participants identified supervisory or management skills as their primary learning interest. Interestingly, clients from the local community chose computer instruction most frequently; this is an intriguing discovery considering that over 80% of our community clients were adults over 35 years of age and approaching the "computer age" for the first time. Many individuals also expressed an interest in content areas not currently available in the Learning Lab: foreign languages, financial planning, study skills, math review, business writing and presentation skills.

In line with their original interests, most conference participants actually worked with management-related learning materials as shown in Table 8.2. Community clients, on the other hand, chose computer instruction programs most often.

The question of who these self-directed learners were is an interesting one. The nature of the Learning Lab allows individuals to self-select for this learning experience, and just who are the adults who come forward? Our demographic data reveal only information about sex, age, and educational level. The majority of conferee and community clients were between 36 and 55 years of age, but we observed that more women than men (63% to 37%) used the Learning Lab, in the conferee group. While 48% of conferee participants had a high school education, in the community group high school and graduate school education was equivalent (35% and 35%).

Based on our observations, the concept of "learning readiness" is a valid one to use in describing adult self-directed learners. Some individuals expressed genuine doubt about their ability to make their own learning choices and evaluations, although all our clients have had educational experience with the pedagogical approach in high-school and college. Perhaps their lack of early preparation in learning how to learn is the dominant influence, as Houle (1980) suggests. The complexity of clients' responses to a self-directed learning process suggests the inherent validity of the type of multi-dimensional developmental instructional model discussed by Kasworm (1983).

Table 8.1: Percentage of Learning Lab Clients with Learning Interests in Different Content Areas[a].

	CONFEREES	FACULTY/STAFF	COMMUNITY
Computer Training	20%	100%	29%
Management	27%		18%
Career	12%		29%
Self-Improvement	13%		12%
Sales Skills	9%		

[a]Nineteen percent of conferees and 12% of community clients expressed an overall interest in the Learning Lab.

Table 8.2: Percentage of Different Categories of Learning Materials Chosen by Learning Lab Clients.

	CONFEREES	FACULTY/STAFF	COMMUNITY
Computer Training	15%	100%	59%
Management	61%		22%
Career	7%		15%
Self-Improvement	8%		4%
Sales Skills	10%		

As she suggests, individuals appear to vary widely in their behavior/skill levels, their operating level of cognition, and personal values attached to learning and acquiring knowledge. Perhaps the idea of a continuum of self-directedness, dependent on such factors as "learning-to- learn" skills, self-awareness of personal influences on knowledge, and a personal belief in the value of learning, would be a useful guiding model. Cherem (1987) very briefly describes a similar model of teaching style and learner's maturity, used in management training by Rogers.

The Impact of Instructional Technology. Our observations and the evaluation responses of Learning Lab clients suggest that characteristics of self-instructional resources influence the process and the overall quality of self-directed learning experiences. The four principles we have developed are found in Table 3. Principle 1 reiterates the need to understand the specific population involved in the self-directed learning experience, by surveying their learning interests, requirements, and predispositions.

Principle 2 captures the nature of the impact instructional resources have on the learner's opportunity to individualize the resources and, therefore, the learning experience. It is a tenet of education that all individuals learn in their own personal style, as a function of experiences, intelligence, motivation, age, and ways of perceiving and processing information. We can assume that these variables are at work during self-directed learning, as well. It follows that the embedded features of any particular learning resource, such as those articulated in Table 8.3, will influence the learning process most directly. Therefore, the characteristics of the instructional resources become critical to the success of the self-directed learning experience.

Burham and Seamons (1987), in discussing Verner's (1962) categorizing scheme for educational processes, suggest that the modern educational technology of CAI and interactive video may represent the first "educational devices" to actually influence the nature and process of learning. If they are correct, then such "devices", rather than being considered only important to learning outcomes as Verner stated, may fundamentally alter how learning takes place. The relevancy of their design, therefore, may be critical to process, as well as to the subjective quality of the self-directed learning experience. In our experience, much of the current adult self-directed learning material, in particular, computer- assisted instruction, is inconsistent with andragogical principles of learning. Opportunities to handle materials in limited amounts, to change answers after reflection, to choose only the parts which are new, or immediately

Table 8.3: Instructional Principles Related to the
Development of Self-Directed Learning Opportunities

<u>Principle #1</u>. The content and subject matter of adult learning resources should reflect the documented interests and needs of the specific population served.

<u>Principle #2</u>. In support of individualized learning strategies, instructional resources should offer opportunities for the self-directed learner to **control-manipulate-shape** information to fit his/her personal learning style.
    The following characteristics are identified as critical to this "learner control" issue:

    a.   opportunities to practice new learning immediately;

    b.   feedback on performance at regular intervals;

    c.   adjustable levels of difficulty;

    d.   adjustable pace of presentation;

    e.   control of the sequence of information presentation;

    f.   opportunity to review/correct/repeat information;

    g.   opportunity to exit and reenter program without repetition;

    h.   opportunity to save responses for future use.

Principle #3. The instructional design features of learning resources should contribute to information presentation in such a way as to enhance (not detract from) the learner's ability to process and assimilate the information:

   a.   information should be presented in more than one format (e.g. watching, hearing, reading);

   b.   displays (such as screens) should be easy to read, with an appropriate number of words and graphic images;

   c.   color and graphics should support, rather than distract from, the information;

   d.   instructions should be clear and the learner should know how to respond;

   e.   selection of options should be easy to understand and execute;

   f.   presented information and any support material should be fully integrated.

Principle #4. The presence of a competent facilitator can contribute to the quality of the self-directed learning experience.

---

relevant--these characteristics of adult learning have not been incorporated into instructional design.

Principle 3 refers to the design, or outward appearance, of the instructional material and highlights characteristics we have observed to be important in working with information without distraction or physical discomfort. Hall (1986) in a report on an adult self-directed learning project conducted in England, describes many of the same characteristics in her "design specifications" for instructional resources.

The Learner and the Environment

In the Learning Lab, conference participants, or other client populations, could choose the instructional media form they desired; 79% of the materials used by conferees wore computer-assisted instruction format and 89% of local community clients used CAI or interactive video materials. These figures are confounded, however, by the fact that almost all the training materials for the computer are available in interactive video delivery format.

The two groups differed in the degree to which they considered CAI or interactive video technology helpful to their learning. When asked to choose which of several components of the Lab (CAI, a facilitator, reading materials) were "helpful factors", 79% of the conferees responding answered "CAI"; only 50% of the community population judged CAI as helpful. Both conferees and community clients chose "talking with a facilitator" as a helpful factor (57% and 58%, respectively). The two groups agreed about audiocassettes and videotapes as helpful factors (36% and 33%, respectively).

In an effort to solicit a broader range of responses, this question was made an open-ended one at the end of the first year of operation. The predominant response to the question about "what was most helpful?" was the answer "pacing" or "going step-by-step", from 64% of conferees and 100% of community clients.

The Role of Staff. Principle 4 of Table 8:3 represents our experience with the uses made of the on-site facilitator in fostering self-directed learning. More important than interviewing skills is the ability to recognize the current perspective of the client and match description to that perspective. Also of great importance is the ability to encourage some level of self-directed activity in the hesitant adult with little belief in their ability to choose and use learning materials wisely, by themselves. Listening skills are important; we observed that the appreciation of personal assessment and personal choices encouraged adult learners to explain the context of their learning needs and plans. All these experiences suggest that the general notion of differences in self-directed "readiness", however defined, has face validity when viewed within the context of individual learners' descriptions of their independent learning attempts and successes.

The Learning Process. All clients were asked to indicate what their "next step" would be, following this learning experience. Of the conferees who responded, 34% wrote that they planned to complete the particular instructional package they were working on, at the next available opportunity. Only 18% of responding community clients mentioned that they intended to complete their work at a future time. Out of the small academic faculty/staff group, 25% planned to complete their work in the future.

Fully 34% of conferees wrote that their next step was to implement or apply what they had learned; only 6% of community clients made a similar statement. Both conferees (22%) and community clients (18%) mentioned taking a course as their next step.

What we observed during initial interviews with a variety of clients is that, while most mentioned a particular topic of interest (management skills, communication techniques, learning about the IBM, for instance), far fewer were specific about the nature of their learning. In other words, most adults described their need, and often mentioned the context (typically, job-related), without describing any particular plan, or series of steps, as articulated by Tough (1979) and his idea of the "planned learning project". It is, of course, possible that the newness of the Learning Lab explains part of the lack of observed planning; Caffarella and O'Donnell (1987) in their recent review report that the existence of self-directed learning projects in Western middle-class populations, at least, has been verified. Future developments in the Learning Lab include expanding the opportunities to facilitate self-directed learning plans, using models similar to that of Stubblefield (1981).

Our observations also suggest, however, that discrete environmental events, such as a promotion or the purchase of office computers, appear to trigger expressions of independent learning. Clients expressed pleasure in discovering such a facility for independent learning at the very time they needed to learn something new, bringing to mind Spear and Mocker's (1984) concept of "organizing circumstances". Other investigators, in a similar vein, have discussed the notion of "timing" as important to adult informal, self-directed learning, meaning that self-directed learning is important to making education fit the needs of the individual, on and off the job (Goldstein, 1986; Sexton-Hesse, 1984).

Quotes from our own clients suggest the serendipitous nature of their self-directed learning:

> ". . . this material on stress was just what I needed to hear right now! It's really helped me see what I've been doing . . ."
> "This goes right along with the way I analyze my time management . . . I'm going to take this (printout) to my boss!"

Perhaps the broadest perspective on the relationship between the self-directed learner and the learning environment is that represented by Brookfield's (1986) term "praxis", meaning the balance of activity and reflection during self-directed learning, or Mezirow's (1985) "perspective transformation". Even without coining new vocabulary, other authors have appreciated that the concept of an individualized learning process should include some type of cognitive change, in perspective, meaning or value system, to separate it from training or education processes. The notion of a balance struck between what is understood and what is not understood may well be at the heart of understanding how adults go about changing, or learning, in completely idiosyncratic ways. The experience of this incongruency (Kasworm, 1983), a non-linear process of change (Danis and Tremblay, 1987), may represent the truly "adult" form of self-directed learning Brookfield has discussed.

Our current observations in the Learning Lab are time-limited and, hence, we have not witnessed long-term examples of "self-directed changing". However, our future plans include the type of follow-up which can reveal the types of changes our clients are experiencing as their learning continues.

The Learning Lab and its Future

Future development of the Lab is planned to allow the achievement of each of the goals described in the first section of this paper. In 1989 the Lab will occupy approximately 3400 square feet in the newly built addition to the Georgia Center, adjacent to both the Center

Library, with a circulation of 4000 volumes, and the video/film Library. With this increase in space comes the opportunity for increasing the number of individual workstations, the inventory of instructional materials, the necessary equipment, and additional staff.

The Lab will expand its delivery modes by offering access to a selection of information databases and bibliographic services, and provide instructional materials via forms of telecommunication technology to distant sites. An effort to utilize the enormous resource environment of the University will include the development of a mentoring system, whereby learners can work with individual content experts.

Efforts to observe and record self-directed learning experiences will be expanded to include scheduled follow-up studies, surveys of Lab users with respect to particular design questions, and efforts to probe the individual learner's personal changes during self-directed learning.

REFERENCES

Brockett, R. G. (1985). The relationship between self-directed learning readiness and life satisfaction among older adults. Adult Education Quarterly, 35, 210-219.

Brookfield, S. D. (1986). Understanding and facilitating adult learning. San Francisco: Jossey-Bass Publishers.

Burnham, B. & Seamons, R. A. (1987). Exploring the landscape of electronic distance education. Lifelong Learning, 11(2), 8-11.

Caffarella, R. S. & Caffarella, E. P. (1986). Self-directedness and learning contracts in adult education. Adult Education Quarterly, 36, 226-234.

Caffarella, R. & O'Donnell, J. (1987). Self-directed adult learning: a critical paradigm revisited. Adult Education Quarterly, 37, 199-211.

Cherem, B. (1987). Situational leadership. A model for teaching adults and managing employees. Online--The Newsletter of the American Association for Adult and Continuing Education, October, 5(4), 8.

Danis, C. & Tremblay, N. A. (1987). Propositions regarding auto-didactic learning and their implications for teaching. Lifelong Learning, 10(7), 4-7.

Dixon, N. M. (1985). The implementation of learning style information. Lifelong Learning, 9(3), 16-18, 26.

Evan, M. J. (1987). Why adults learn in different ways. Lifelong Learning, 10(8), 22-25, 27.

Guglielmino, L. M. (1978). Development of the self-directed learning readiness scale (Doctoral dissertation, University of Georgia, 1977). Dissertation Abstracts International, 38, 6467A.

Goldstein, H. (1986). Timing of the educational process. In J. N. Burstyn (Ed.) Preparation for Life? Philadelphia: The Falman Press, 147-153.

Hall, D. (1986). Adult learning by choice. Results of the CET Learning Links Project. Council for Educational Technology, ED 277816.

Houle, C. O. (1980). Continuing learning in the professions. San Francisco: Jossey-Bass Publishers.

James, W. & Galbraith, M. (1985). Perceptual learning style: implications and techniques for the practitioner. Lifelong Learning, 8(4), 20-22.

Kasworm, C. (1983). Self-directed learning and lifespan development. International Journal of Lifelong Education, 2(1), 29-45.

Knowles, M. S. (1975). Self-directed learning. New York: Association Press.

Knowles, M. S. (1980). The modern practice of adult education: From pedagogy to andragogy. (2nd edition) Chicago: Follett.

Korhonen, L. & McCall, R. (1986). The interaction of learning style and learning environment on adult achievement. Lifelong Learning, 10(2), 21-23.

Mezirow, J. (1985). A critical theory of self-directed learning. In Stephen Brookfield (Ed.) Self-directed learning: From theory to practice. San Francisco: Jossey-Bass Publishers.

Sexton-Hesse, C. (1984). Assuming responsibility for self-directed learning in professional practice: the contribution of psychosocial factors. Proceedings of the twenty-fifth annual Adult Education Research Conference, 202-207.

Spear, G. E. & Mocker, D. W. (1984). The organizing circumstance: environmental determinants in self-directed learning. Adult Education Quarterly, 35(1), 1-10.

Stubblefield, H. W. (1981). A learning project model for adults. Lifelong Learning, 4, 24-26.

Tough, A. (1979). The adults' learning projects. (2nd edition) Toronto: Ontario Institute for Studies in Education.

Verner, C. (1962). A conceptual scheme for the identification and classification of process. Washington, D.C.: Adult Education Association of America.

Bridging Theory

Chapter Nine

THE CONTRIBUTION OF W.H. KILPATRICK'S WORK (1918) TO ADULT SELF-DIRECTED LEARNING THEORY

Charlene A. Sexton

In the 1960's, two studies were conducted which provided the impetus for investigations of self-directed learning (Houle, 1961; Johnstone and Rivera, 1965). Tough's study (1965) of the self-teacher emphasized the adult as primarily responsible for planning and maintaining motivation for learning. Self-directed learning now constitutes one of the most frequent topics of adult education research (Brookfield, 1984).

However, scholars have noted the inadequate conceptualization in this body of research (Chene, 1983; Kasworm, 1984; Brookfield, 1984; Spear and Mocker, 1984). Kasworm (1983) and Oddi (1987) argued that personality appears to be a central factor in self-directed learning. A recent study confirmed the potential of a developmental personality perspective (Sexton, 1985).

More rigorous empirical research is one approach to resolving the conceptual ambiguity surrounding this phenomenon. Another approach is to examine it from a historical perspective. Is self-directed learning unique to the conditions of modern society and restricted to adult education thought? Have previous educators formulated similar ideas?

The purpose of this paper is to demonstrate that the roots of self-directed learning theory are partially in the project method and child-centered foci in American curriculum theory, as exemplified in the work of William Heard Kilpatrick. A disciple of Dewey and faculty member at Teachers College, Kilpatrick proposed the organization of curriculum around children's purposes (projects) rather than around subject matter.

There are three sections of this paper. The first section describes the development of the project method concept in Kilpatrick's thinking. This development took place in the context of competing curriculum reform ideas dominating the early twentieth century. The second section examines Kilpatrick's article, "The Project Method" (1918). The publication of the article brought the project method concept to the pinnacle of American curriculum theory. The third section of the paper discusses how Kilpatrick's concept of project method is instructive to adult education research of self-directed learning. In this regard, questions will be raised about conducting historical research within the broad framework of American educational thought.

THE PROJECT METHOD: ITS PLACE IN KILPATRICK'S PERSONAL AND SOCIAL WORLD

William H. Kilpatrick was a school teacher, principal, then professor of mathematics at Mercer University in his native Georgia before joining the Teachers College faculty in 1909. He received his Ph.D. from Columbia University in 1912 and remained on the Teachers College staff until his retirement in 1938. He died in 1965 at the age of 94.

In his position at Teachers College, Kilpatrick initially taught history of education. This complemented his dissertation work, a historical study of The Dutch School of New Netherlands and Colonial New York (1912). He was later responsible for teaching educational theory, which stimulated his analysis of pedagogical theories (The Montessori System Examined, 1913; Froebel's Kindergarten Principles Critically Examined, 1916).

The interests and motivations inspiring Kilpatrick's writing of "The Project Method" are partially apparent in his work prior to 1918. He took a graduate course at Columbia University with Dewey, who was then formulating his general method of problem solving, presented in How We Think (1910). However, it was the experience of teaching countless education theory classes which led to an increasing concern about identifying educational methods which promoted coherent practice. In the introduction to the article he states: "I had felt increasingly the need of unifying more completely a number of important related aspects of the educative process" (pp. 319-20). The writing of the article presented Kilpatrick with the opportunity to articulate this unifying concept, which he called "project." The term, project, was certainly not new in educational literature: "I (Kilpatrick) did not know how long it has already been in use" (p.320).

Interestingly enough, the term was used twenty years earlier in the literature of vocational agriculture. Rufus W. Stimson, a teacher at Smith's Agricultural School in Massachusetts, had implemented the "home-project plan" in his classes. He used the plan to bridge the subject matter presented in class with his students' experiences in living and working on the farm. Based on their home-project plans, students introduced new agriculture procedures learned in class, and sometimes even earned money for their work (Kliebard, p.155).

By 1911, only three years after the home project plan's initial implementation, the idea began to receive national attention. The U.S. Commissioner of Education asked Stimson to prepare an article for the Bureau of Education Bulletin. Other governmental departments published articles on the idea. F.E. Heald, a U.S. Department of Agriculture specialist, wrote, "The Home Project as

Phase of Vocational Agriculture" in 1918, the very year Kilpatrick published his article. Heald emphasized that the major factor in the home-project was "the personal interest of the pupil...(and that) the immediacy of motive has a considerable bearing on the final success (of the home project)" (in Kliebard, p.156).

This viewpoint contradicted that of Charles Prosser, who asked Heald to prepare an article on the subject. Prosser, the Federal board of Vocational Education's Director of Executive Staff, saw value in home-projects because they prepared students for agricultural employment and contributed to economic development. Prosser and Heald's views of the home-project are particularly striking because their fields, vocational education and vocational agriculture, are somewhat related. Their opposing views attest to the upheavals in educational thought occurring in the early twentieth century, and especially to the divergent opinions about the curriculum which were held by otherwise like-minded educators.

Who were the major curriculum reform groups of that period, and to which group did Kilpatrick and other home-project educators align themselves? Which groups, if any, supported the ideas presented in Kilpatrick's article? As seen in Table 9.1, four groups competed for national leadership in reforming school curriculum. The questions they raised became rallying calls for reform proposals advanced by persons who often became leaders at the national level. Traditionalists like William T. Harris, who shared the conceptual orientation of the nineteenth-century mental disciplinarians, focused on curriculum content in relation to strengthening mental faculties like memory and reasoning.

The viewpoints of the other curriculum reform groups departed quite radically from the traditionalist viewpoint. The social efficiency reformists, led by persons like David Snedden, focused on the social aims of education. If the curriculum prepared the student to earn a living and thus additionally promoted national social and economic development, it was adopted. The scientific curriculum reformers, led by Charters and Bobbitt, raised entirely new questions: How can the curriculum be organized to promote efficient learning and teaching? The developmentalists also had an altogether new focus: the learner and the social environment. G. Stanley Hall and Dewey, who led educators' explorations into psychology, social philosophy, and the metaphysics of experience, triggered a decidedly child-centered approach in the developmentalist group.

The child-centered approach of the developmentalist curriculum reform group was clearly compatible with the orientation of educators like Kilpatrick who were interested in the project method. These project method educators, who were initially restricted to vocational education and vocational agriculture settings, grew to include those in elementary and secondary school settings. For example; in 1916 science educators began publishing General Science Quarterly, a journal which promoted the project method as a means of reforming science teaching. In the lead article for the journal's first issue, Dewey criticized science teaching for ignoring the child's level of development and understanding. Reflecting the developmentalist's child-centered approach, he urged teachers to view science from "the standpoint of pupil's experiences of natural forces together with their ordinary useful applications" (in Kliebard, p.158).

Table 9.1: Kilpatrick's Project Method in Relation to the Curriculum Reform Groups of 1915-1935

Reform Group	Curriculum Question	Reform Focus
1. Traditionalists	1. What is to be learned?	1. Subject matter
2. Social Efficiency Reformists (D. Snedden, G. Counts)	2. What purpose does learning serve?	2. Educational Aim
3. Developmental-ists (G.S. Hall, J. Dewey)	3. Who is the learner; what are the learner's interests?	3. Educational Process
4. Scientific Reformists (W.W. Charters, J.F. Bobbitt)	4. How can learning best be organized?	4. Subject Matter Organization
The Project Method (W.H. Kilpatrick)	What unifies the important aspects of the educative process?	Learner's Purpose(s)

These events were propitious for Kilpatrick in two ways. They further stimulated him to write "The Project Method" article, and they triggered shifts and realignments among the competing curriculum reform groups around the project method. The social efficiency, developmentalists, and traditionalist groups found the project method appealing for quite different reasons. The scientific curriculum reform group was cautious, if not outright rejecting of the idea. The article further stimulated the diffusion of the idea, while implicitly rejecting the orientation of educators like Charters and Bobbitt:

> He (Kilpatrick) seems to have struck in his proposal a deep well-spring of opposition to the scientific curriculum-makers whose hardline efficiency and scientifically determined standards represented newly dominant ideals in curriculum matters (Kliebard, p. 162).

Thus, when Kilpatrick's article was published in 1918, "it literally catapulted him to national and international fame. Over 60,000 reprints were destined to circulate during the next twenty-five years" (Cremin, pp. 216-17). Not only was this overwhelmingly positive reception to the article a boon for Kilpatrick's career, but it was "Without a doubt, the single most dramatic event in the evolution of the movement to reform the curriculum through projects" (Kliebard, p. 159).

ANALYSIS OF "THE PROJECT METHOD"

The preceding section of the paper illustrates the prominent place of the article in the evolution of Kilpatrick's theorizing, as well as its contribution to curriculum theory. For these reasons alone, it is worthy of careful analysis. However, it is the thesis of this paper that analysis is also warranted because the self-directed learning theory in adult education shares aspects of the conceptual orientation presented in the article. This orientation was modified and expanded in Kilpatrick's later works (1925, 1935, 1941).

The foundation of Kilpatrick's orientation is a concept called "project." In the educational literature of his time, "project" had a variety of meanings which created confusion and misunderstanding. Some educators were outright scornful of the idea, while others tentatively accepted it. Kilpatrick's intent was "to attempt to clarify the concept underlying the term (and) to defend the claim of the concept to a place in our educational thinking" (p.321). He was therefore clear at the outset about his meaning of project. It is, he wrote, "wholehearted purposeful activity proceeding in a social environment, or more briefly, in the unit element of such activity, the hearty purposeful act" (p.321).

Because of the confusion surrounding the term, Kilpatrick provided examples of project:

> ...a pupil writing a letter, a child listening absorbedly to a story...DaVinci painting the Last Supper, my writing this article, a boy solving with felt purpose an 'original' in geometry (p.321).

These examples demonstrate that "project" encompasses a wide variety of activities, indeed, as various as are the purposes in life. Realizing the dilemma, he attempted to delimit the concept. All are examples of wholehearted purposeful activity, "if we think of project as a pro-ject, something pro-jected" (p.321). A striking feature of his description is its distinctly psychological orientation. He emphasized that "a mere description of outwardly observable facts might not disclose the essential factor, namely the presence of a dominating purpose" (p.321).

In this regard, Kilpatrick had two caveats. He advised that individuals vary in the degree of dominating purpose, or wholeheartedness, with which they pursue an activity. Consequently project is an ideal activity; it can only be approximated and never fully realized. Secondly, he foresaw that the social aspect of his orientation would be ignored or eliminated because of the emphasis on purpose. He underscored its significance by stating: "(the project) demands the social situation both for its practical working out and for the comparative valuation of proffered projects" (p.322).

Why was Kilpatrick so insistent on a psychological and social element in his conceptualization of project? Recall that he was looking for a concept to unify educational practice. If the concept was to serve this purpose, then it had to meet certain conditions. The concept must:

1. "emphasize the factor of action."

2. "provide a place for the adequate utilization of the laws of learning."

3. "provide a place for the essential elements of the ethical quality of conduct."

4. "provide for the important generalization that education is life" (p.320).

These conditions require consideration of the individual and learning from both psychological and social perspectives. For example, utilization of the laws of learning (condition 2) refers to matters like perception, motivation, readiness, all of which are in the psychological domain. Providing for the ethical quality of action (Condition 3) is clearly in the social domain.

Educational practice during Kilpatrick's time ignored these psychological and social perspectives. Instead, the dichotomies felt to exist between thinking and feeling, idea and action, individual and society, produced an educational practice which Kilpatrick deplored:

> It is the thesis of this paper that these evil results must inevitably follow the effort to found our educational procedure on an unending round of set tasks in conscious disregard of the element of dominant purpose in those who perform the tasks (p.328).

The conceptualization of project was an attempt to ameliorate these dichotomies by developing an approach which unified the psychological and social dimensions of learning as it occurred in real-life situations outside the school. His article is essentially an argument for and illustration of improved educational practice when it is based on these interrelated dimensions of learning.

Accordingly, Kilpatrick provided a classification of types of projects ensuing from four kinds of purposes (see Table 9.2). All projects, except for the second type, could be executed through the following steps: purposing, planning,

Table 9.2: Kilpatrick's Classification of Projects

PURPOSE (Steps)	PROJECT	PROCEDURE
1. "to embody some idea or plan in external form."	-building a boat -writing a letter -presenting a play	purposing, planning, executing, and judging
2. "to enjoy some (esthetic) experience."	-listening to a story -hearing a symphony -appreciating a picture	
3. "to straighten out some intellectual difficulty or solve some problem."	-finding out whether or not dew falls -ascertaining how New York outgrew Philadelphia	purposing, planning, executing, and judging
4. "to obtain some item or degree of skill or knowledge."	-writing grade 14 on the Thorndike Scale -learning the irregular verbs in French	purposing, planning, executing, and judging

executing, and judging. Kilpatrick had no definite procedure for guiding projects involving aesthetic experiences. He acknowledged his indebtedness to Dewey and McMurry in formulating the third type of project (problem solving) and the steps for conducting the projects.

The schema and the very choice of terms he used reflects the instrumentalist and pragmatic philosophical view pervading educational thought in the early twentieth century. Knowledge was not simply to be stored, but to be used. The use of knowledge was significant for two reasons: it enhanced the pupil's thinking process and moral development. Both of these ideas were critical features of Kilpatrick's conceptualization of project, and had special consequences for the role of the teacher.

Like Dewey, Kilpatrick employed the homeostasis model of thinking in which the individual first experiences some difficulty or problem and then seeks its resolution or understanding. In addition, he drew upon E.L. Thorndike's educational psychology, which views learning as the strengthening of stimulus-response bonds. Within the framework, he argued that educational activity begins with the child's own purposes, with subject matter employed for the accomplishment of those purposes. Rather than the teacher being in the forefront of educational activity selecting curriculum content and organizing experiences (for which he was critical of the Montessori Method), he saw the role of teacher as that of evaluator:

> Motive and occasion arise together; the teacher has but to steer the process of evaluating the situation. The teacher's success-if we believe in democracy-will consist in gradually eliminating himself or herself from the success of the procedure (pp. 329-30)

On what basis does the teacher evaluate the procedure as successful or not? If it leads to growth and expansion of interests, for example, if "a skill acquired as end can be applied as means to new purposes" (p. 331), then the activity is successful. Genuine educative activity has an expansive, "leading on" quality in his framework. He was unequivocal about this:

> ...the criterion of the value of any activity-whether intentionally educative or not-is its tendency directly or indirectly to lead the individual and others whom he touches on to other fruitful activity (p. 328).

Kilpatrick clearly places the criterion for educative activity within a social context. A project, by leading on to other interests which have social ramifications, enhances the child's moral development. Therefore, knowledge was useful in promoting moral development as well as thinking. In this framework, the special role of the teacher is not that of content expert, but social expert. "It is the special duty and opportunity of the teacher to guide the pupil through his present interests and achievements into the wider achievement demanded by the wider social life of the older world" (pp. 328-29). As social expert, the teacher is able to use the social group in mediating between social demands and individual interests.

The ideas which Kilpatrick presented in his article, although favorably received, did not go uncriticized. William C. Bagley, a colleague at Teachers College, declared that the entire project method rested on too many untested assumptions and concepts. Some members of the various reformist groups also rejected the idea of using the project method rather than subject matter as the basis of the curriculum. The most persistent and studied critic was Boyd H. Bode at Ohio State University. Bode found the idea of "purposeful activity" indistinguishable from interest. He shared Dewey's hesitation about reconstructing the curriculum on the project method function. The basis of their criticism was a profound skepticism "of the fundamental developmentalist assumption that the key to the question of what to teach lay in the unfolding of natural forces within the child" (Kliebard, p.177).

IMPLICATIONS FOR ADULT EDUCATION RESEARCH

How is Kilpatrick's conceptualization of "project" instructive to adult education research of self-directed learning? First, it demonstrates that self-directed learning theory, which began to surface in adult education literature in the 1960s did not originate at that time. The adult education concept, "learning project," was rapidly diffused in the 1970s through the works of Tough and others. Its conceptual beginnings are evident decades earlier in the literature of American secondary education.

Second, an analysis of Kilpatrick's "Project Method" article reveals that "project method" and "learning project" are more related than a mere similarity in terminology suggests. There are many parallels in the conceptual orientation formulated by Kilpatrick and those formulated by Tough and others. Both orientations are decidely psychological. Dominating purpose and "whole-hearted, purposeful activity" are the underpinnings of Kilpatrick's conceptualization. "Learning project," defined as "an intentional change, a highly deliberate effort" to learn (Tough, 1979,p.1), also has a psychological orientation.

A third and perhaps most important way that the project method concept is instructive to adult education research is through the conceptual clarity which arises from examining two related conceptual frameworks. Isolating the differences between frameworks often permits researchers to recognize ambiguities and problems which may otherwise have gone undetected. An historical perspective aids the process of isolating differences and identifying important variables, thus contributing to the generation of new and better conceptual frameworks.

There are three differences project between method and learning project which are noteworthy. Kilpatrick views the project method as contributing to moral development and democratic citizenship. This is not addressed in the framework of learning project. A professional who undertakes a learning project which has an ethical dimension might well be involved in a process of moral development, and not just professional development.

Second, Kilpatrick places special emphasis on the task of judging, one of four steps in the project method. The matter of judging is crucial because of the social as well as personal outcomes of the activity. This is not addressed in the framework of learning project. Instead, deciding and planning the project are the decisive steps.

Third, Kilpatrick proposes a continuum of project method activity, ranging from those which are more coerced ("compulsive acts") to those which are more "wholehearted." The psychological value of the activity increases the more purposeful the act. In the learning project framework, the focus is on self-directed activity, determined by the number of hours involved in planning. Examination of these and other differences offer much potential for the development of sound self-directed learning theory in adult education.

REFERENCES

Brookfield, S. (1984). Self-directed learning: A critical paradigm. Adult Education Quarterly, 35, 56-71.

Chene, A. (1983). The concept of autonomy in adult education: A philosophical discussion. Adult Education Quarterly, 34, 38-47.

Cremin, L.A. (1961). The Transformation of the school: Progressivism in American education, 1876-1957. New York: Alfred A. Knopf.

Dewey, J. (1910). How we think. Boston: D.C. Heath.

Houle, C.O. (1961). The inquiring mind. Madison: University of Wisconsin Press.

Johnstone, J.W. & Rivera, R.J. (1965). Volunteers for learning. Chicago: Aldine Publishing Co.

Kasworm, C. (1983). Self-directed learning and lifespan development. International Journal of Lifelong Education, 2(1), 29-46.

Kilpatrick, W.H. (1912). The Dutch School of New Netherlands and Colonial New York. (Unpublished Doctoral Dissertation, Teachers College, Columbia University, New York).

Kilpatrick, W.H. (1914). The Montessori System examined. New York City: Teachers College Bureau of Publications.

Kilpatrick, W.H. (1916). Froebel's kindergarten principles critically examined. New York City: Teachers College Bureau of Publications.

Kilpatrick, W.H. (1918). The project method. Teachers College Record, 19, 319-35.

Kilpatrick, W.H. (1925). Foundations of method: Informal talks on teaching. New York: Macmillan.

Kilpatrick, W.H. (1935). A reconstructed theory of educative process. New York City: Teachers College Bureau of Publications.

Kilpatrick, W.H. (1941). Selfhood and civilization. New York: Macmillan Co.

Kliebard, H.M. (1987). The struggle for the American curriculum: 1893-1958. London: Routledge & Kegan Paul.

Oddi, L.F. (1987). Perspectives on self-directed learning. Adult Education Quarterly, 38, 21-31.

Sexton, C.A. (1985). Self-Directed Learning in Professional Practice: The Relationship Between Eriksonian Psychosocial Factors and Assuming Responsibility for Learning. (Doctoral Dissertation, University of Wisconsin-Madison, 1985). Dissertation Abstracts International, 47, 759A.

Spear, G.E. & Mocker, D.W. (1984). The organizing circumstance: Environmental determinants in self-directed learning. Adult Education Quarterly, 35, 59-71.

Tough, A. (1965). The teaching tasks performed by adult self-teachers. (Doctoral Dissertation, University of Chicago, 1965).

Tough, A. (1979). The Adult's learning projects: A fresh approach to theory and practice in adult education (2nd Edition). Toronto: Ontario Institute for Studies in Education.

Chapter Ten

TRUTH UNGUESSED AND YET TO BE DISCOVERED: A
PROFESSIONAL'S SELF-DIRECTED LEARNING

Huey B. Long

Wilder Graves Penfield became the 1,645th entry in The Penfield
Genealogy when he began his life in 1891. Born on January 26 he was
the third child of Charles and Jeannie Jefferson Penfield. The older
siblings included a brother Herbert, born in Bucyrus, Ohio and a sister
Ruth who, like Wilder was born in Spokane. Seven years separated
Wilder and Ruth who was born in 1884. Herbert's exact date of birth
is not revealed, but it was late 1882 or early 1883.

The Penfield family lived in Spokane until 1899 where Charles'
practice as a physician provided a comfortable life. Wilder's first
seven years of life in Spokane appear to have been normative with
little to distinguish him from other Spokane children of the period
except for two factors. First, the child became more aware of his
father's absences from home and his practice. Increasingly Charles
turned to the western wilderness for escape from the dominance of
Jean. As a result the appearance of a normal life began to
deteriorate. Second, Jean's efforts to substitute young Wilder as an
object of her love and attention created an extremely close
relationship between mother and son that lasted until her death, and
beyond.

In 1899 the family was torn by the decision that sent Jean,
Herbert, Ruth and Wilder back to the maternal home in Hudson,
Wisconsin. Penfield's biographer describes the family's arrival in this
manner:

> On a bright, crisp November day in 1899 when the family
> stepped off the train in Hudson Wisconsin, Wilder was eight
> years old, a slender boy with fine, light brown hair, light blue
> eyes and already a distinctly stubborn jaw. He was energetic
> and intense and very self-conscious, as quick to anger as to
> laughter. 'It would be a terrible responsibility to bring Wilder
> up' his sister, Ruth, noted in her diary in 1900, 'because he is
> such a firefly and is so willful-and yet he is very affectionate
> and easily led.' (Lewis, 1981, p.17)

The next ten years of Wilder's life were nurtured in Hudson, a town of about 4,000 nestled against the eastern bank of the St. Croix River. It was typical of many towns of its day. Fortunes were slow and hard to come by. Relationships were established according to custom and social level. Recreation was simple and religion was important. Success was associated with hard work and self-denial. Wilder's position in the community was determined, in large measure, by the fact that his grandfather, Amos Jefferson, was the town banker.

The Bible and the Protestant church were significant elements in Wilder's life. As a small boy he developed the understanding that important things were unchanging, and that if he read his Bible, worked hard and obeyed the golden rule, he could grow up to be anything he liked. This was the well spring of that certainty and confidence that distinguished him in adult life.

However, Wilder's separation from his father created for him a problem of relationships with older men. He developed a mistrust of them and had some difficulties with Amos Jefferson, Jean's banker father. The difficulty in relations with older men possibly contributed to the continuing strength of the relationship between mother and son. Well educated, Jean filled many of Wilder's hours with poetry, moral and religious instruction and a sense for the romantic.

Jean appears to have reason to have been more than satisfied with her efforts. In the absence of his more easy-going father, Wilder developed into a young man who alternated between a healthy, boyish delight in pranks and jokes, sports and games and a serious, self-conscious moralism that mirrored his mother's.

In 1904, soon after his thirteenth birthday, Wilder began to keep a diary, the start of a lifelong habit. The diary provides an interesting and informative view of the developing young Penfield who continued to have difficulties in accurately assessing his errant father and the implications of his father's actions for Wilder's relationship with other men.

Wilder's diary, the Galahad School, a dream of a Rhodes Scholarship and his strong Christian faith provided the foundation for the next ten years of his life. At least three of those four elements were inspired by Jean. In 1904 she heard a student talk about his Rhodes Scholarship and she quickly planted the ideas in Wilder's head. Next, to provide the kind of educational foundation he would need, she provided the leadership needed to create a private school in Hudson. The school, known as the Galahad School was opened in 1905 in a large two-story stone house sitting on ten acres of land two miles from Hudson overlooking Lake St. Clair. His Christian faith supported him during days of indecision concerning his future profession. Perhaps as a reaction against his father, he early rejected medicine and thus restricted his professional options to law or the ministry. Despite lack of clarity concerning the specifics of his future he had no doubt that God had a mission for Wilder Penfield and anyone else who was willing to listen to him. He needed only to remain patient and open.

At sixteen, strongly convinced he would become a minister, he is attracted to Helen Kermott. Standing on the precipice of life at sixteen the world can be a foreboding challenge or a provocative opportunity. Thus, with mixed emotions Wilder departed for Princeton in 1909. Wilder's first impression of Princeton was consistent with his expectations; he was filled with awe and delight. Soon he became an active member in the Philadelphian Society, an unaffiliated Christian undergraduate society until the mid-1870's when it became one of the first college Y.M.C.A.'s. Through the Philadelphian Society Wilder formed most of his friendships.

Wilder's first term at Princeton is typical of his approach to life's many challenges. First, he resolved some of the problems of finances. He learned that he could save $100 per year through a remission of tuition if his lodging expenses in his dormitory apartment were less than $150 for each term. By using only one electric light rather than the four installed in the apartment he kept the expense to $148.50. Next, he turned to his athletic goal of being a member of the Princeton football team. He soon discovered he was one of sixty candidates for the team. And many of the older aspirants were bigger and had played for large eastern prep schools. In his efforts to become a first string player he emphasized the concentration, extra effort and determination that he had learned in Hudson. He also learned how one's acceptance by others was associated with status such as team membership. During these trying days he also discovered that he was stretching himself too much to accomplish his academic goals. He wrote to his mother that he must decide to join an Eating Club or to devote himself to the grind of study. He doesn't reveal his choice, but it seems as if he chose to devote more time to study. Yet, he found time after Christmas to become a member of the wrestling team. Wilder's commitment to the demanding schedule he adopted rested squarely on his assumption that one day he was going to be somebody. It was also at this time in his life that his opinions were important in his assessment of his life goals and activities. Thus, he began to exert his independence from the influence of Jean and others.

His sophomore year was in many respects a copy of his freshmen year. He prepared for the Rhodes Scholarship exam along with his other pursuits. He had little expectation of obtaining the appointment on his first try so he was not surprised when the board selected another candidate and advised him to reapply his senior year.

Maturity was providing him with other opportunities, however. For example, he discovered that he was less attracted to the ministry. He developed very negative attitudes toward the men he met at the Princeton Seminary that reflected some of his early childhood experiences. He described most of the men there as "sound, but uncultured, ungentlemenly weaklings" (p.36). As a result of his biology course and the inspiration of Edward Conklin he began to more seriously consider medicine as a career. Other experiences such as visiting Presbyterian Hospital with a school chum, who had chosen medicine as a career, impressed Wilder and turned his attention to the possibility of surgery as a career.

In a mental state of crises he determined he had to make a decision concerning his future. Characteristically he found a quiet location in the gallery of the Princeton library. Here, at the top of a sheet of paper, he deliberately and self-consciously wrote "objective: to support myself and family and somehow make the world a better place in which to live" (p.38). Below the statement he developed a list of possible professions. One by one he eliminated them until only medicine was left. So, despite some lingering uncertainty, he seems to have made one of several important decisions concerning his life's work.

Perhaps one of the greatest threats to his choice of professions emerged in the summer between his sophomore and junior years. Back in Wisconsin he renewed his friendship with Helen Kermott. Returning to Princeton he wrote "when I look forward to being a doctor and taking nine more years of preparation it appalls me... the girls I know will all be old before then" (p.39).

His junior year was devoted to strengthening his decision and determination to become an outstanding doctor. He gave up the safety razor in preference for a straight razor to develop a steady hand for surgery. Soon he was shaving with either hand! He joined the newly organized Medical Club and took a variety of courses from history of philosophy to chemistry. At this time he also became interested in psychology. He wrote "it seems to me there might be a good field for a doctor in Psychology" (p.40).

At this time Wilder and several of his friends formed "The Dr. Johnson Society" for the purpose of reading, talking and bickering. The group met each Sunday after prayer meeting. Five of the group continued to meet and share with each other long after their college years were over.

As a senior Wilder turned away from football that had been so important to him three years earlier. He had lettered at tackle and was known as "W.G. Penfield, the football player" (p.42). He merely noted that football was one "mile-post" passed (p.42). Ahead, the Rhodes Scholarship remained. He also had to distinguish himself in his studies.

On a sunny late autumn day he climbed up to the highest level of the fire escape of Edwards Hall to read and reflect. From here he could see the entire town and campus of Princeton. He wrote in his diary: "I felt myself aloof and alone. I fancied I was seeing the towers of the Arts and Sciences in a dreamlike city of the intellect. There was so much more to learn there and, beyond the learnings, there was truth unguessed and yet to be discovered" (p.42).

The key to Wilder's visionary city was the Rhodes Scholarship. To get it he would have to bring his course standing up to the honors level. By Christmas he had succeeded. He was elected "Best All-Round Man," "Most Respected Man" and the student who had "Done Most for the Class Generally." (p.42). Yet, he failed to get the coveted scholarship appointment. The Committee for New Jersey split on a choice between Wilder and Valentine Havens from Rutgers. Havens was finally selected and Wilder was urged to try again the following year with some assurance that he would then be appointed.

Wilder's reaction was a combination of disappointment and relief. For about nine years he had chased the dream. Now he could pass over it and get on with his decision to become a doctor. He was convinced that had he been selected for the scholarship it would not have been a direct route to his goal of becoming a doctor.

Yet, his future medical studies were not guaranteed. His grandfather Jefferson who was the primary source of his support died. He also had conflicting prospects for earning some money to support himself. He had agreed to teach at Galahad in Hudson for a year after graduating from Princeton. After making the commitment he received an offer to coach Princeton's freshmen football team. He wound up doing both. He also obtained summer employment in Nova Scotia as a tutor for the two sons of Dr. J.M.T. Finney of Johns Hopkins.

The next year of Wilder's life was sufficiently complex to challenge the strongest person. His father died. His relationship with Helen Kermott ranged from a near break-up to engagement for marriage, he was offered the envied Rhodes Scholarship without even applying for it and he was offered the head field coaching job for the Princeton varsity football team. In order to not waste time he enrolled at Harvard to study anatomy and Greek in the summer.

His preparation for Oxford reflected Wilder's previously selected method of study. It seems as if his self-perception did not include any ideas of himself as a brilliant scholar. Rather he perceived of himself as a plodder, someone who succeeds only by dint of stubborn and repeated efforts and ferocious concentration that would have to substitute for genius. In the years ahead, he was to develop and follow a carefully cultivated ritual of focusing his entire attention on the topic or problem at hand, forcing himself to shut out anything and everything that was not important, or examining a patient. Some of his rules of study are as follows:

1.   Study in a pool of light

2.   Keep things the same, even if a new way seems easier.

3.   Never waste a minute. (p.47)

Wilder's years at Oxford were critical ones for him as well as the British people. He crossed the Atlantic in January of 1915 and found an Oxford University that had been depleted by the effects of war. He was immediately challenged by academic problems as he planned to spend only two years at Oxford and complete his medical training at Johns Hopkins. Except for the assistance of Sir William Osler his plans might not have been completed. However, armed with an introductory letter from Dr. Finney Wilder approached Osler for help. As a result he took courses at Oxford and then at Edinburgh in the summer.

At Oxford Wilder was challenged and stimulated by Osler who he considered to be the perfect model of the physician and by Sir Charles Sherrington who was, for him, the perfect model of the scientist. The influence of these two giants ultimately contributed to Wilder's decision to join neurosurgery and neurology. At that time a great gulf separated the clinical practice of the neurologists and the surgery of the neurosurgeon.

Forty years later Wilder wrote that Sherrington had influenced his scientific thinking more profoundly than anyone else. It was not however, just the physiological information and the spirit of scientific exploration that Sherrington shared. It was also his deep sense of wonder, and awe, at where it all might lead. Penfield noted "I looked through his eyes and came to realize that here in the nervous system was the great unexplored field-the undiscovered country in which the mystery of the mind of man might someday be explained" (p.57).

Wilder's first Christmas vacation, Dec. 1915, was typical of him. He and some other Americans went to France where he worked in a hospital and performed many duties of a regular doctor, learning by observation and trial-and-error. The experience was so gratifying he planned to spent his spring vacation in France. However, on his way across the English Channel his ship, the Sussex, was torpedoed and Wilder was injured. Wilder's survival, even though severely wounded, was interpreted by him as a sign that he had been saved for some purpose.

At age twenty-five Wilder had completed two years at Oxford. He then returned to Johns Hopkins for two more years of study. He was becoming impatient to marry and get on with his life. During this period of his life his relationship with his mother began to change. Up until this time he had been the recipient of her advice, but more and more she was now turning to him for guidance. It was also at this time and place that he verbalized his interpretation of the relationship between his parents. He perceived that Jean was a very strong woman who could not be led by his weaker father. Helen's role also seemed to have become more important as he increasingly turned to her rather than to his mother. He and Helen were married on June 9, 1917 and spent their honeymoon working in a Red Cross Hospital in France.

In November, 1917 Wilder and his pregnant wife sailed from France for Johns Hopkins where he was to continue his lifelong search. The decision to leave the stimulating surroundings of the hospital and war ravaged France was not an easy one. But, the wisdom of the decision was underscored by older doctors with whom he worked.

Following graduation from Johns Hopkins Wilder served a one year surgical internship at Boston's Peter Bent Brigham Hospital. Shortly afterwards he completed a paper on blood-pressure experiments he had done at Johns Hopkins and it was soon published in the <u>American Journal of Physiology</u>.

During the internship in Boston Wilder had to make more specific decisions concerning his career. He could go into general practice or choose a specialty which would require several more years of study. Partially based on Helen's father's experience they agreed to chose a specialty, but which one?

Typically, Wilder sought a place of peace and quiet when he had to make an important decision. He addressed the decision of a medical specialty in much the same way he had first chosen medicine as a profession some years earlier. Only now he substituted a cottage at the Rhode Island sea shore for Princeton's library gallery. He decided on brain surgery partially as a result of assisting Dr. Harvey Cushing who was considered the best brain surgeon in the world. While working with Cushing Wilder would come home at night and fill notebook after notebook with his observations of Cushing's innovative techniques and making notes to himself on how he thought they could be improved.

Wilder, however, had interests along lines that differed from Cushing's. Cushing was primarily interested in patients with brain tumors and neuralgia. Penfield continued to be influenced by the memory of Sherrington's undiscovered country. Thus, Wilder, began to consider the need for additional study of neurosphysiology that could be linked with Cushing's innovative procedures. He reasoned that he needed to know all that could be known about the human brain, neuropathology, neuroanatomy, neurocytology, then go on to clinical neurosurgery and finally develop the operative techniques of neurosurgery.

Penfield's view was novel for the time and represented a significant departure from traditional approaches that dominated the specialities of that day.

From the time Wilder returned to Oxford in 1919 he began a lifetime of self-designed study that would build upon his earlier practices of observation, reflection and concentration. One of his most important achievements of the year of graduate study was how to carry out research; an accomplishment that he quickly added to his arsenal of learning skills.

Thus, Wilder's illustrious career proceeded on a system of self-directed learning. He often traveled along a road not previously taken and had few who could provide directions. When he did discover someone whose expertise could be applied to problems of his specialty he lost little time or effort to plumb their knowledge. Ramon y Cajal was such a person. In 1923 Wilder's efforts to discover an improved method for staining brain cells were at a dead end until he turned to Cajal. In the fall of 1923 armed with a Spanish dictionary he studied Cajal's procedures as reported in documents in the New York Academy of Medicine. Yet, the procedures he introduced did not yield uniform results. In March of 1924 he departed for Spain where he could study the method directly with Pio del Rio-Hortega who had extended Cajal's procedures.

Later, after an illustrious career and hundreds of carefully conducted inquiries in the surgery and laboratory he joined forces with Herbert Jasper to study and develop the application of electroencephalography, EEG for short. Use of the EEG for diagnostic purposes was much more effective than the electrical probe previously used.

In the 1930's Wilder turned his attention to considerations that normally were beyond the concerns of the neurophysiologists. His interest in the human brain led to a theorizing about the location of a "transformer" or "switchboard" that transformed that gross action of the cortex to subtle, dexterous movements of the concert pianist or the skillful graceful movements of the ballerina. In essence his questions moved from those that concerned the brain to those that focused on the mind.

He revealed his search for understanding in the following quotation from the twenty-eight chapter of Job he used in the preface of a paper presented in 1938: "Surely there is a vein for the silver and a place for the gold where they find it...But where shall the wisdom be found? And where is the place of understanding? (p.202)

Eventually Wilder's search for understanding along the boundaries of science, philosophy and religion led to the development of theories of explanation, models for testing and conjecture for stimulation. In his latter years he was projecting his interest in the mind to questions of the should and how to best use his talents.

On a vacation to Greece, he made the following entry as he typically used his diary to wonder how "to use my present talent and training and the place and influence that have come to me, for good. I can speak, if I work hard on the text. I could write, I suppose, as well as ever, or better. I can study new material, though slowly (when wasn't I slow?). I can reason more maturely, and I think, soundly. At 77 I could labor hard at something for 3 or 6 or even 10 years (p.293).

Almost desperately searching for a mission to complete in the winter of life he discovered two final projects. One was an autobiography entitled No Man Alone and the other was a final analysis of his research, philosophy and faith. It was a culminating desire to determine what he had discovered, what he believed and some speculations about the role of science in understanding the human spirit. His biographer describes the work as not a scientific book, but a statement of faith.

To the end, Wilder kept his most frequently used tool of learning, his diary, with him. Only a short time before his death on April 5, 1976 he made his final effort to understand. The last phrase written in a thin, shaky hand was merely "Here I am..." (p.304).

ANALYSIS

There is little doubt that Wilder Penfield was a self-directed learner. His life reveals a number of interesting possible traits or characteristics that may be associated with self-direction in learning. Let us look at some of the more conspicuous elements as follows:

1. Self confidence

2. Self-awareness

3. Self-reflection

4. A strong goal orientation

5. Systematic procedures

Self Confidence
At times it is possible Penfield's self-confidence may have been hard for his friends and acquaintances to handle. Yet, the source of his confidence was his deep Christian faith and his belief that he was destined to make a major contribution to science and humanity. As a consequence, his occasional periods of self-doubt were not as pessimistic as they may have been otherwise. His faith provided him with the opportunity to have humbling questions about specifics in his future, but not with the eventual general outcomes.

Self-Awareness
A realistic appraisal of his abilities served to counter the development of over confidence. He reveals that he did not think of himself as being a genius or overly intelligent. Yet he believed that he could overcome the negative consequences of being average or above average by effort and concentration.

Self-Reflection
His diary provided a mechanism for self-reflection. Here he could focus his self-awareness and his self-confidence on specific problems and develop procedures for solutions.

Strong Goal Orientation
Penfield's life can be described as a process of achieving a series of goals. His first major life goal was to obtain a Rhodes Scholarship. Others of varying degrees of importance are discovered among the mileposts of his journey toward the undiscovered. He was determined to be a varsity football player. He was committed to strengthening his academic credentials. He planned his medical studies to accommodate his financial planning, matrimonial goals and eventually his career objectives. He studiously considered the implications of a general practice and a specialty. With eyes open he chose a career

path that was non-traditional and insecure. He identified problems of diagnosis and technique and searched for their resolution.

Systematic Procedures
Early in his adolescence Wilder Penfield discovered the value of systematic and organized procedures. First, he found that writing and concentration on problems were productive activities. Gradually he refined these activities so that he sought isolation, light, efficiency and systematic efforts in his study efforts whenever appropriate. Yet, he never rejected the importance of learning from others. He carefully observed experts such as Cushing and Ramon y Cajal and translated their efforts into notes and diagrams that he later improved upon. He seems to have generally valued criticism and suggestions from experts and colleagues. Much of his scientific writing was collaborative. He was especially sensitive to advice when his scientific activities reached toward philosophical and religious boundaries. Despite his sensitivity to the advice of others, he ultimately accepted the final responsibility for his beliefs, conjectures, hypotheses and conclusions.

Conclusions
Penfield's life as a self-directed learner suggests several hypotheses concerning critical elements in self-direction in learning.

1. Self-directed learning is associated with self-confidence.

2. Self-directed learning is associated with self-awareness.

3. Self-directed learning is associated with self-reflection.

4. Self-directed learning is associated with a task or goal orientation.

5. Self-directed learning is associated with systematic procedures.

Wilder Graves Penfield was a pioneer neurosurgeon who was one of the first scholar-practitioners to combine the study and practice of clinical neurology and neurosurgery. In the 1920's many of the problems and questions in neurosurgery required an inquisitive and highly disciplined approach.

Two objectives guided the analysis of the biography of Wilder Penfield: (a) to determine how he approached the general learning tasks encountered by living; and (b) to identify specific characteristics of his self-directed learning.

Penfield's biography reveals he purposely and intensely addressed learning tasks he considered to be important. His life story also indicates he developed some specific procedures to learn. These procedures are identified in the paper.

In a larger sense the results of this study imply biography in general may be a useful and stimulating source for studying adult self-direction in learning. For example, Penfield's adult self-directed learning practices followed a pattern he established as a youngster. Studies of multiple biographies could conceivably suggest some generalizations concerning life span development of self-directed learning.

REFERENCES

Lewis, H. (1981). Something hidden: A biography of Wilder Penfield. Ontario, Canada: Doubleday.

DATE DUE

DEMCO 38-296